D1255177

The Simple Truth

The Simple Truth

FOR YOUR BUSINESS

Why Focused and Steady
Beats Business at
the Speed of Light

by Alex Brennan-Martin

OWNER OF BRENNAN'S OF HOUSTON AND
COMMANDER'S PALACE, LAS VEGAS

and Larry Taylor

AUTHOR OF *BE AN ORANGE*

BRIGHT SKY PRESS
340 South 2nd Street
Albany, Texas 76430
www.brightskypress.com

Text copyright © 2003 by Alex Brennan-Martin and Larry Taylor
Cover illustrations © The New York Public Library

All rights reserved. No part of this book may be reproduced in any form,
brief excerpts for the purpose of review, without written permission of the publisher.

10 9 8 7 6 5 4 3 2
Library of Congress Cataloging-in-Publication Data

Brennan-Martin, Alex, 1958-
    The simple truth / Alex Brennan-Martin and Larry Taylor.
        p. cm.
    Includes bibliographical references.
    ISBN 1-931721-36-X (alk. paper)
    1. Success in business—United States. 2. Customer services—United States—Management.
    3. Personnel management—United States. 4. Restaurant management—United States.
    5. Industrial management—United States. 6. Brennan's of Houston (Restaurant)
    I. Taylor, Larry, 1950- II. Title.

HF5386.B825 2004
650.1—dc22

Book and cover design by DJ Stout and Erin Mayes, Pentagram, Austin, Texas
Printed by Capital Printing, Austin, Texas

Dedication

TO EVERYONE AT BRENNAN'S OF HOUSTON FOR PUTTING UP with me as I took this journey; most especially to Carl Walker, friend and partner of a lifetime. To my family: my sister, Ti, Lally, Brad and Aunt Dottie. To my mom Ella for prodding me to get this done and for being the best parent and mentor anyone could ever have. To Joe and Ted for your invaluable counsel and friendship. To the guys of Forum V, thanks for not laughing at me when I said I was going to write this book, and for your unconditional support and friendship. To Mark, Karen and Cullen, my family of choice. Most importantly to my ladies and my loves: Lexie, Addie and Jane... if y'all ever leave me I'm going with you!

—ALEX BRENNAN-MARTIN

AS I HAVE DEDICATED MY LIFE TO HER, I DEDICATE THIS BOOK to my beautiful wife, Laura. She has always held me up even in those times when I have let her down.

—LARRY TAYLOR

Acknowledgments

WE WOULD FIRST LIKE TO THANK RUE JUDD OF BRIGHT SKY PRESS for having confidence in us and making it possible to bring our ideas to life in this book.

Lisa Grey, our editor, made us sound much more eloquent and coherent than we really are! Erin Mayes and DJ Stout of Pentagram for a fabulous design that made our vision come to life.

Contents

INTRODUCTION

Why Did I Do This to Myself? 14
BY ALEX BRENNAN-MARTIN

Southern Hospitality in Las Vegas? The Proof is in the Bread Pudding 18
BY LARRY TAYLOR

FIND YOUR SIMPLE TRUTH

Understanding the Simple Truth 24

Complex Businesses, Simple Truths 27

    WAL-MART'S SIMPLE TRUTH

    WALT DISNEY WORLD'S SIMPLE TRUTH

    KING COUNTY METRO'S SIMPLE TRUTH

    KROGER'S SIMPLE TRUTH

The Milestones on the Journey 32

My Journey Begins 33

The Big Meeting 35

The Three Communities 38

    CUSTOMER EYES

    THE EMPLOYEE'S POINT OF VIEW

    HOW YOU SEE YOUR SELF

The Search 43

How You Ask *44*

What You Want to Know *47*

Your Business's Simple Truth *48*

Hurdles *52*

    CUSTOMER HURDLES

    EMPLOYEE HURDLES

Your Secret Ingredient *56*

Prices and the Secret Ingredient *60*

Your Lagniappe *64*

    PERSONAL LAGNIAPPE

    COMMUNITY LAGNIAPPE

Delivering the Simple Truth *67*

Staying on Track *70*

Asking Customers *73*

Asking Employees *78*

THE POWER OF PLODDING

The Tortoise and the Hare *83*

Why Focused and Steady Beats Business at the Speed of Light *84*

The Core Beliefs of Plodding *87*

    EVOLVE, DON'T CHANGE

    MAKE EVERYBODY HAPPY

    MAKE THE RIGHT CHOICE

    THE VICIOUS CYCLE VS. THE VIRTUOUS CYCLE

Minding Your P's and Q *93*

    PROFIT

    PEOPLE

    PRIDE

    QUALITY

Getting Started *101*

    KNOW WHAT YOU'RE COOKING BEFORE YOU PICK YOUR POT

    CLEAN THE REFRIGERATOR

    GET BUY-IN SOMEWHERE

    TALK ABOUT IT

Leading a Plodding Organization *107*

    IT BEGINS WITH FOLLOWSHIP

    DON'T TAKE RESPONSIBILITY. GIVE IT.

    TRUTH AND TECHNOLOGY

    RELEASE THE WATER UNDER THE BRIDGE

    NEVER ASK MY OPINION

    TEACH, DON'T TRAIN

    DRIVE-BY MENTORING

    GUIDE TO A SUCCESSFUL MEETING WITH ALEX

    ONE TRUTH, ONE SCORECARD

WHY HOSPITALITY MATTERS

Getting Connected *124*

    HOSPITALITY IN A GLASS

    HOSPITALITY IN A STORM

The McDonald's Syndrome *128*

Puttin' on the Ritz *131*

HARNESS HUMAN NATURE

The Power of Human Nature *136*

    WHAT PEOPLE WANT

    WHAT'S IN IT FOR ME?

The Need for Connection *140*

    THE 359-DEGREE CIRCLE

    DON'T HIRE SUPERSTARS OR INDIVIDUALS

SINK RUSTY SHIPS

SOME JUST HAVE TO EXPERIENCE IT

SOMETIMES EXPERIENCING IT ISN'T ENOUGH

Plan for the Worst 150

PRIZE PATROL

White Space Planning 155

You Can Feel It Working 158

LAGNIAPPES

Larry's Lagniappe: A consultant examines Brennan's culture 162

Alex's Lagniappe: An Intimate Conversation with Alex and Ella 169

Plodding Is Never Finished 176

Introduction

Why Did I
Do This to Myself?

BY ALEX BRENNAN–MARTIN

"What the world needs is more geniuses with humility;
there are so few of us left."
— OSCAR LEVANT

I LIVED WITH CHAOS, WAS A ONE-MINUTE MANAGER, TRIED TO out-do Deming, zeroed in on zero defects, moved my cheese, continually improved on continuous improvement, reengineered my engineering department, and attempted every trend that could be labeled with three letters

These books were valuable and inspirational. My restaurant, I thought, was the perfect lab to test all those theories. Every day, we mix hundreds of people with different interests, backgrounds, and needs. We force them together in high-pressure situations in which everyone has high expectations and low levels of tolerance. Good restaurants make that business look easy. The best make it look effortless.

Keeping up with business trends, though, was anything but effortless for me. I began each experiment full of hope, but at the conclusion was always left with an empty feeling in my stomach. Something was missing or not quite right — and maybe, I thought, maybe the next new theory would fix it. At one point, I had to keep a yellow card in my pocket to remind me which new initiative I had adopted that week. If I was that confused, imagine my poor staff — busy serving customers while I searched for miracle cures.

I should note that by most people's standards, my business was healthy. Brennan's of Houston turned a reliable profit — an impressive feat for a mature restaurant in a competitive city. Customer counts were fine, and profits were growing at a nice pace. But I wanted more: more profits and more satisfaction. I wanted to make my mark.

I knew how good a restaurant could be. I'd grown up in the kitchen of Commander's Palace, one of the most acclaimed restaurants not only in New Orleans but in all of America. My mother and her family owned the place and ran it passionately. In my twenties, I studied the restaurant business in France with the legendary chef Roger Verge. In Manhattan, I worked in the Four Seasons restaurant as well as the original Maxwell Plum.

The restaurant business was my birthright, part of my soul, as much a part of me as New Orleans. So why, I wondered, was I struggling at age 40 to find the business solution that would take my business from acceptable to extraordinary?

I was pondering that question one spring afternoon five years ago during a Burgundy moment on the patio at Brennan's of Houston. I looked at the wine in my glass, and it hit me: Wine, a complex beverage, has been made pretty much the same way for centuries. Great winemakers use modern technology, but they don't abandon their heritage and traditions while doing it. Even in the third millennium, the same basic process yields the finest wine!

The idea was a blinding flash of the obvious. I remembered a quote I'd heard earlier in life: "He was so busy learning the tricks of the trade, he forgot to learn the trade."

My family had taught me the business, but I was spending my time studying new tricks. Maybe those empty feelings I was having were not in my stomach, but between my ears. Each new process didn't feel right because it wasn't right. It wasn't the way I had been raised, and it wasn't the way I had built a successful restaurant business.

It was a defining moment. I realized that I needed to get back to the basics. I had to stop acting like a child chasing lightning bugs and find a simple business philosophy that I could master, rather than one that would master me.

At last, I had found the miracle cure I was looking for — and it wasn't a miracle at all.

Since I began focusing on the basics, my business has thrived, even by my standards. During the last five years, our profitability and reputation have improved more than I thought possible. Not only has Brennan's of Houston held its own against many newcomers, it has outperformed many of its traditional competitors. We have kept more of the employees who deliver what our customers want and made room for others like them. Good former employees have returned — perhaps one of the best signs that we are on the right track.

I've also helped my family open a restaurant in an entirely new city — Commander's Palace of Las Vegas. Its success proved that my method can be replicated.

I'm not saying that I've been to the mountaintop and seen the light. And I'm not Jack Welch — just a small businessman who finally figured out why his business had been stuck for years.

But I've shared my methods with my customers, peers, and other business leaders, and their feedback shows that the strategies that have worked for me will work in any business — whether it's selling shoes, real estate, stocks, insurance, or drill bits. The ideas are basic.

Just as people ask for recipes of their favorite dishes at Brennan's of Houston, many business friends asked me to put down on paper what I learned from my return to the business basics. But this is not a restaurant book, nor does it contain any recipes.

The Simple Truth is about what I learned in my effort to make the old hard-won ways work today and endure (while remaining flexible) well into the future. The book explains how to marry tradition with enlightened ways of dealing with technology and people. And it chronicles a journey of self-discovery that I took with my staff and customers.

Not every item on my menu would be right for you. In the same way, not everything in this book is right for you and your business. I encourage you to modify (or even reject) the ideas and to make the ones that work for you your own.

I hope you find this book as tasty as the dishes we prepare for our guests. Life is short; eat well!

Southern Hospitality in Las Vegas? The Proof Is in the Bread Pudding.

BY LARRY TAYLOR

"A friend is a person before whom I may think out loud."
— RALPH WALDO EMERSON

I HAVE BEEN A FRIEND AND CUSTOMER OF ALEX'S FOR MORE THAN 20 years. Whether I first became a customer or a friend, I cannot remember. In Alex's world, the two relationships are seamless.

One spring morning, Alex asked me to meet him at Brennan's of Houston for a free lunch. I agreed to a time and date before he could change his mind.

I'm a management consultant, and at lunch we settled into one of our usual conversation veins. We talked about management, operating issues and business concepts — the things that make businesses succeed.

Through the years I have benefited greatly from my discussions with Alex, so I wasn't surprised when he told me he was thinking about writing a book about his approach to management. "What do you think?" he asked. "Should I do it?"

We began discussing ideas for the book. Alex brought out a tattered piece of paper with a rough outline, showing the points he wanted to make.

Then he asked me if I'd co-author the book. "You've written a couple of business books; you understand my business, and you work with all different types of businesses, so you can see how my concepts can translate to other businesses."

Quicker than accepting a free lunch, I told him I'd be honored. We toasted the new relationship with glasses of sweet tea.

Since clearly defined roles are important to successful teamwork, Alex and I determined that I would be the writer and the synthesizer. Although the book would be a collaboration, we decided to use Alex's voice to tell the story.

Our writing sessions were lively discussions of ideas and approaches. Alex talked about his experiences and lessons, then I embellished the ideas and organized them into a manuscript form. We met to edit and polish.

We agreed that the book would have to prove that the philosophy not only works for other businesses, but that its success could be replicated, and that what works for Brennan's of Houston is not an anomaly. Luckily, as we were beginning this book, he was also planning and opening his family's new restaurant, Commander's Palace in Las Vegas, three states away.

Though Alex and his family had opened many new restaurants, this was the first time the venerable Commander's Palace name had appeared outside New Orleans. Commander's Palace is a Southern institution. Why in the name of Andrew Jackson, I wondered, had he picked Las Vegas, a city with no heritage and no reverence for Southern tradition?

Vegas is as plastic and neon as New Orleans is old and humid.

As a friend, I worried. But as Alex's co-author, I was delighted. Opening in Las Vegas would be the ultimate test of his philosophy.

One year after the Las Vegas Commander's Palace opened, the proof was in the bread pudding — or actually, in the February, 2002, "Best Restaurants" reader survey in *Las Vegas Life* magazine.

Commander's Palace stole the show! Readers voted it "Best Restaurant on the Strip," "Best Overall Restaurant in Las Vegas," and "Best Service in Las Vegas." And here's what the magazine had to say:

> *No matter where you sit in this elegant establishment — be it the light and airy Garden Room, the intimate Parlor, or the more boisterous Wine Room, you are sure to be pampered by one of the smoothest wait staffs in the city. It could be plain old Southern hospitality, but service here manages to be both gracious and unobtrusive. The staff performs so smoothly and efficiently — whether it's replenishing the bread or placing the entrees — which you barely notice. Kudos to the Brennan family.*

There are few times in business that you know, really know, that something has worked. This was one of those times. The people of Las Vegas had spoken; Alex's Simple Truth philosophy had met the challenge. He had assembled over 100 Las Vegas people, many of whom had never even been to New Orleans. His philosophy helped them not only act with Southern Hospitality, but to understand it, know why it matters, and be accountable for their performance.

We all like to eat delicious food, and we all like to dine in great restaurants. And as business people, we all like to learn how to be better at what we do. I guarantee that if you will see the restaurant examples in this book as metaphors for your business, you will come away with solid ideas that can improve your business. And you will make more money.

I suggest that you use that extra money to fly to Houston, Las Vegas or New Orleans to experience Southern hospitality and treat yourself to a great dining memory.

Be sure to tell Alex that I sent you.

Find Your Simple Truth

Understanding the
Simple Truth

"Talent without discipline is like an octopus on roller skates.
There's plenty of movement but you never
know if it is going backwards, forwards or sideways."
— H. JACKSON BROWN JR.

IN *ALICE IN WONDERLAND*, WHEN ALICE ARRIVES AT A CROSS-road the Cheshire Cat asks, "Where do you want to go?"

Alice replies, "Why, I don't know."

"Then any road will do," says the Cheshire Cat.

Five years ago I found myself at Alice's crossroad. Before I could decide the best road for my business to take, I had to ask what I wanted my business to be.

Obviously, I'm in the restaurant business. If you looked up the phone number for my business, you would find it listed in the *Houston Yellow Pages* under "restaurants" — along with 4,595 other restaurants. If we produced an annual report, you would learn that Brennan's of Houston has often been listed in the Top 100 independent restaurants in America, and one of the highest "reader poll rated" restaurants in the city. We employ about 100 people and have served over five million customers.

With a little research you would also learn that my family has enjoyed success in the restaurant business for more than

50 years. My mother, Ella Brennan, is part of the Brennan's family in New Orleans, and is an owner of Commander's Palace, which is consistently rated the number-one restaurant in New Orleans by Zagat and has won just about every hospitality-industry award possible.

But like you, I am not in the restaurant business.

And in reality, you are not in the business of selling cars, building buildings, making widgets, trading stocks, or whatever the *Yellow Pages* publishers think you do.

After much soul-searching, I concluded that I was taking the same path that all restaurateurs were taking. All my competitors believed they were in the business of preparing and serving gourmet-quality meals to discriminating diners. It was a crowded path which made it difficult for my restaurant to stand out. I needed to find a new path — one that was my own, one that separated my business from the pack, one that allowed my restaurant to stand out and to be outstanding.

That search eventually led me to understand what I call the Simple Truth of my business.

The Simple Truth answers the three most important questions in your quest for excellence and success:

☞ What is the real product my customer is buying?
☞ What special ingredient differentiates my product?
☞ Why is my customer really buying what I am selling?

The Simple Truth is more a feeling customers have than an object they can see, but it is very real to them. *The Simple Truth* taps into the emotional connection that consumers have with the brand.

Arriving at the Simple Truth means truly understanding what business you are in, why you are in business, and how you will deliver a value-added point of difference to your customers.

The Simple Truth brings laser-sharp focus to every decision you make because it is the unadulterated essence of why your business exists and the most sacred belief by which all decisions are made.

The Simple Truth will set you free.

Complex Businesses,
Simple Truths

*"Whenever you see a successful business,
someone once made a courageous decision."*
— PETER DRUCKER

BEFORE I DESCRIBE MY OWN JOURNEY TOWARD DISCOVERING
the Simple Truth of our restaurants, let me first highlight the
Simple Truths of four other organizations.

WAL-MART'S SIMPLE TRUTH

*"The point of philosophy is to start with something
so simple as not to seem worth stating, and to end with something
so paradoxical that no one will believe it."*
— BERTRAM RUSSELL

Wal-Mart did not get to be the largest retailer in the history of
the world by letting others define its business. A recent *Fortune*
article on Wal-Mart reveals Wal-Mart's Simple Truth: "To lower
the world's cost of living."

Everything Wal-Mart does flows from that core idea. Every
decision made in Bentonville or Biloxi or Beaumont aims to
lower the world's cost of living. That's why store managers are
given the power to lower prices but not to raise them.

WALT DISNEY WORLD'S SIMPLE TRUTH

"Imagination is the beginning of creation. You imagine what you desire, you will what you imagine and at last you create what you will."
— GEORGE BERNARD SHAW

Walt Disney World probably understands its Simple Truth better than any other company. Disney World is not in the theme-park business, or even the entertainment business; it is in show business.

Employees are called cast members, and they refer to being at work as "being on stage." The personnel department is called "Casting Center." Cast members do not wear uniforms — they wear costumes, and they are not allowed to go onstage unless they are totally in character.

Like most businesspeople, I am awed by how the Disney organization trains its people and consistently delivers a quality experience. Disney World has a staff 42,000. Some 80 percent of them come into direct contact with the customer. It is estimated that the Disney World employees have 10 million moments of truth with customers each day.

Several days of training ensures that every employee knows that what he is doing is putting on a show. Even the cleaning people understand that they are actors. Disney World research shows that people with brooms are five times more likely to be asked questions than the people designated to answer questions.

You can't leave the Simple Truth to management. It's for the whole team.

KING COUNTY METRO'S SIMPLE TRUTH

"No matter where you go, there you are."
— BUCKAROO BANZAI

In Seattle, King County Metro Transit is not just in the bus business; it is in the business of delivering mass transit so enticing that it lures people from their cars. Its safety record is one of the best in the nation. Its stations are sparkling clean, its vanpool and regional ridematch programs are easy to use and highly successful; and its 1.3-mile electric bus tunnel under Seattle was completed both ahead of time and under budget. Employees love their jobs and stay with them; absenteeism is only 2 percent, about five times less than in San Francisco.

King County Metro shows that Simple Truth can energize even a government agency.

KROGER'S SIMPLE TRUTH

"Better by far that you should forget and smile than that you should remember and be sad."
— CHRISTINA ROSSETTI

Bob Zincke has been my friend and loyal customer for many years. As president of the Southwest division of Kroger Food Stores, he is responsible for 212 stores in Texas and west Louisiana.

Why has Kroger's market share in Houston share grown from 17 percent to 31 percent over 10 years? I believe it's because the Kroger team understands their product and has a simple way to keep the team's focus.

If you ask Bob what his product really is, he will quickly tell you it's "smiles." He's in the "smile store" business, not the grocery-store business.

"From our research," Bob says, "we have found that the price of our grocery products is what most often gets us in the shopper's 'considered set' of stores, especially with new customers. But we have also found that as long as we have competitive prices, our customers maintain a high level of loyalty.

"We know that when our customers have a positive experience in our store, especially during the check-out process, they not only keep coming back, but they are not as easily swayed by our competitors who try to build their business on cheap prices. Someone can always sell at a lower price, but can they build a loyal customer base on price alone? We know they can't.

"It's real simple. If the customer leaves happy, she will come back. If she's not happy, we may not see her again. So our leadership team's task was to articulate this strategy in terms that a 16-year-old part-time sacker could understand and use to make decisions under the pressure of the shopper staring at them.

"We created the term 'smile store' and spent a lot of time teaching our people what it means. But even the employee who has never before worked in a grocery store can understand our product and his or her role in consistently delivering that product to a customer. If it makes her smile as she walks out the door, you did your job. If she's not smiling, your job is to figure out why, and then do something about it."

Bob told me about a coaching opportunity he had with a sacker. Remember that shoppers decide whether to come back based on how they are treated at the front of the store where the sackers reside. And sackers are often the lowest-paid, youngest, and least-motivated employees.

Bob saw a sacker put a six-pack of beer in a bag. He placed it on top of a loaf of bread, and the frustrated customer called the error to the sacker's attention. Fortunately, a customer service manager also saw the incident and immediately ran to get the customer a fresh loaf of bread. But what would have happened had the customer service manager not been there?

After the customer left, Bob took the sacker aside. He asked whether the customer smiled when he put the six-pack on top of the bread. The sacker quickly replied, "No."

Then Bob asked if she smiled when he put the six-pack on bottom and the bread on top. The sacker thought for a couple of seconds. Then the light came on. "Yeah," he said.

"Your primary role is to make sure the customer leaves with a smile," Bob told him. "Pay attention to what makes her smile and do more of it." And that's all that Bob or any Kroger manager needs to say to maintain the integrity of the product that Kroger really sells.

The Milestones
on the Journey

*"You've got to think about the big things while you are doing the small
things, so that all the small things go in the right direction."*
— ALVIN TOFFLER

YOU WON'T FIND YOUR SIMPLE TRUTH OVERNIGHT OR AT A
one-day strategic-planning retreat. It is a journey — a journey
through the "mind fields" of your customers and employees.

The scariest part of the journey is that it requires you to test
your beliefs about yourself and honestly evaluate your own performance. *The Simple Truth* is a customer-focused strategy, but it
includes strategic insights into employees and the owner or
manager who I'll refer to as "self."

There are three basic milestones on the journey:

☞ Being brutally honest with yourself
☞ Seeing your business through "customer eyes"
☞ Understanding your core communities

My Journey Begins

"There are no shortcuts to anyplace worth going."
— BEVERLEY SILLS

YOU'D THINK THAT I, OF ALL PEOPLE, WOULD UNDERSTAND MY own business. But the process took me many years.

I was still in short pants in 1967, when my family opened Brennan's of Houston, modeled on Brennan's of New Orleans. The combination of excellent food and elegant surroundings quickly captured the attention of Houston's underserved restaurant patrons.

But in the early '70s, competition grew stiff, and our restaurant lost some of its luster. Brennan's of Houston continued to make money, but it was resting on its laurels.

I arrived in Houston in the mid '80s, and I did the expected. I tried to make the restaurant "new" again.

First, I tried a hip approach: a TV commercial featuring that icon of modern dining, Andy Warhol. (Let's not dwell too long on that moment.)

When that failed, I tried the next predictable route, menu tinkering. I took some great Creole dishes and tried to make them "more hip" to appeal to the leg-warmers-and-aerobics *Flash Dance* crowd. We take great pride in reinvigorating classic Creole dishes and breathing new life into them but they are still Creole at thier roots. Creole food lovers don't like fads!

I followed the pack and added Nouvelle Cuisine, but that didn't last either. (The legendary French chef Paul Bocuse was right when he said, "Nouvelle Cuisine usually means not enough on your plate and too much on your bill.")

No matter what wonder foods we added to our menu, turtle soup, pecan trout and bananas Foster remained our best sellers. I resented my customers' lack of sophistication. How could they not see that what we were doing was extraordinary?

The '80s oil bust devastated Houston's restaurant business and left me with time on my hands. I read *In Search of Excellence* and *Reengineering the Corporation*. I tested other business philosophies.

Customers didn't seem to notice. The staff met my miracle cures with lethargy. My resentment and frustration were palpable.

I hit bottom in 1998. When I realized my business-trend books weren't working, I did what managers in trouble always do. I called a meeting.

The Big Meeting

"There is a time for departure even when there's no certain place to go."
—TENNESSEE WILLIAMS

ALL MY SENIOR TROOPS WERE GATHERED IN THE ROOM WHEN I sat down. The atmosphere was no different from any of hundreds of previous meetings — the kind where we talked and postured and left the room with a false sense of accomplishment.

We began by discussing sales results and performance. I was angry and more disengaged than usual. My frustration infected everyone.

I sat silently observing the chaos and bickering. With no plan but to stop the insanity, I halted the meeting and went around the table asking each person the same question: "What is your job?"

Each manager gave a reasonable, straightforward answer: "I take care of the front of the house," "I'm the purchasing agent," "I'm responsible for our waiters," "I'm the banquet manager," "I'm the executive sous chef, so I'm responsible for the dinner, kitchen crew, and specials."

The realization hit me like a Mike Tyson punch.

Not one person had mentioned the customer. Nothing about how they interacted with the customer. No one even used the word "customer" in his response. Each person had his own turf, and it was clearly being marked in the meeting. No wonder they were bickering!

That moment I understood what I had never before allowed myself to understand. They were all doing what I had hired them to do, manage, fix things, cook food, and buy stuff. I had hired them and trained them, and they were doing exactly what I had told them to do.

As I caught my breath, I also realized that I was a large part of their frustration. I had told them they were hired to do one thing, but I held them accountable for something entirely different. I preached that we should take our direction from the customer, but I forced them to take their direction from me.

When it came to my turn, I had difficulty speaking. I was simultaneously depressed and exhilarated. They had just laid out for me the vital ingredient to meeting customer needs, a common purpose that mattered equally to everyone, something beyond a paycheck, something that they could believe in and to which they wanted to belong.

I asked the group, "Who hasn't been mentioned?" They looked to see who was absent.

Finally someone muttered, "The customer?"

It was as if the chef's soufflé had fallen. Everyone stared at the table, not wanting to make eye contact with anyone in the room, least of all me. The silence was deafening.

For the first time, I acted like a leader rather than an owner. I told them that I, too, had not mentioned the customer. The customer had not even entered my mind until we had gone all the way around the table.

I admitted that I had failed them. I had not done my job of focusing on the customer because I, too, was focused on doing my job. I had not defined what I do in customer terms any more than they had. I defined what I do by tasks rather than by customer outcomes. I had viewed myself just as I viewed them, as cogs in a machine.

At last, I opened the door to the breakthroughs I had been dreaming of for years. The very fact that I had openly admitted my responsibility and failings came as a relief to my key people.

As they shuffled out of the room, I had another moment of clarity. I recognized that I had been far too busy managing the business to see that I really wasn't managing what made the business succeed — the people.

Even if I had the best chefs, managers and support team possible, until they worked together to give the customer what really mattered most to him, we would forever be doomed to the cycle we were in, a cycle that none of us enjoyed. We were wasting energy on things customers did not care about one whit, and I was the one orchestrating the mess.

My job as the leader became clear, to understand what really matters to our customer. Then make that the only objective by which we make decisions and measure our performance.

That realization changed my business. And my life.

At that meeting — the one that my team now calls "The Big Meeting" — I did two things right then. First, I admitted there was a problem. Then I admitted I was the root of the problem.

Time and again in my years as an owner and manager I had made assessments while wearing my "need-to-prove-I'm-always-right" filter. Concluding that my business was broken didn't threaten me. That was easy to do.

But it threatened my very soul to admit that I, the owner, could be part of the problem. I did not get on the right path until I admitted that I was not only part of the problem, I was the epicenter of it.

The Three Communities

"Listen or thy tongue will keep thee deaf."
— AMERICAN INDIAN PROVERB

IT'S OBVIOUS THAT THE CUSTOMER SHOULD BE THE FOCUS OF a business. But the customer is just one community that must be considered for a business to operate at its peak performance level, and to consistently deliver on its Simple Truth.

Being customer-focused actually means focusing on all the people who contribute to the customer experience. To be successful, a business must equally meet the needs of three communities:

- Customers
- Employees
- Self

CUSTOMER EYES

"A guest sees more in an hour than the host in a year."
— POLISH PROVERB

Success lies in the eyes — in your ability to see your business through the eyes of the people you serve.

Many years ago, when I was being schooled in the family trade at Commander's Palace, I was giving the main dining room one last check before opening the doors to our customers. I walked around like a proud admiral inspecting his fleet. The dining room looked perfect to me.

Bob, a veteran gray-haired waiter, motioned me to a table where he was seated. "Come sit down," he said.

I tried to ignore him, pretending I was occupied with higher duties. But he persisted, and not wanting to be rude, I did as he asked.

He didn't say anything, but gazed around the dining room. Curious, I did, too. After a moment, I noticed burned-out bulbs in two recessed light fixtures and matchbooks being used to level three tables. Walking past them, I hadn't noticed anything. Seated at the table like a customer, I had a totally different perspective.

"Always see what your customer sees," the waiter said softly. "I call it 'customer eyes.'"

Mike Vance, the former president of Walt Disney University, tells a similar story about his legendary boss, Walt Disney.

A Disneyland park attendant once spotted Mr. Disney down on his hands and knees. The attendant ran to his boss and said, "Oh, Mr. Disney, are you OK? Let me help you up!"

Disney got up under his own power and dusted the knees of his pants. "Son, I'm fine," he said. "I'm just looking at my product from the perspective of my customer!"

What we see and how we think is totally influenced by our perspective. Only when you see your business from the customer's perspective can you see the problems and the solutions.

Remember — the eyes have it.

THE EMPLOYEE'S POINT OF VIEW

*"Accomplishing the impossible only means
that the boss will add it to your regular duties."*
— DOUG LARSON

You cannot deliver the Simple Truth unless the employees understand the Simple Truth. The customer is *numero uno*, but until the employees' needs are aligned with those of the customer, there is an inherent conflict. In the heat of battle, employees will respond based on how they feel, not how they were told to respond.

Management's "aha moment" may not seem significant to people down the line — because the employees in direct contact with the customer already know in their guts what the customer wants. They feel the heat of a disenchanted customer and bask in the glow of a happy one. When management doesn't understand the Simple Truth, it causes friction between employees and management.

Many of our valuable customer insights come through the front-line employees. Not only do they hear more customer comments, but they hear those comments through different ears than does the boss or owner.

Our challenge is to get them to share those insights with us, to believe that we want to know. Employees may know the Simple Truth already, but they need management to lead it.

Employees enjoy satisfying customers. It makes them feel good about their jobs and about themselves. That solid base of self-esteem enables people to deliver the Simple Truth under pressure, and more importantly, to go the extra step to make sure the customer leaves with a smile and the desire to do business with you again. It's a virtuous cycle.

Stew Leonard's, a family-owned grocery-store chain in Connecticut and New York, is acclaimed for satisfying both its customers and its staff. The store makes its staff's needs a top priority. Says President and CEO Stew Leonard, Jr., "If you look after your staff, they will look after the customer who will look after your profits."

HOW YOU SEE YOUR SELF

"Growth demands a temporary surrender of security."
— GAIL SHEEHY

I call the third community "self" rather than "you." I believe that to be a peak performer you need a strong sense of self and an accepting view of yourself.

As you feel about yourself, so you will perform.

Performing at your highest personal level can happen only when you have quiet confidence. It's the serenity of achievement combined with feeling comfortable in your skin. It's feeling sure that your direction is sound and truthful, and that it can withstand the tests of both time and turbulence. It's living an authentic life.

Your personal needs must be met for you to be fulfilled at your job. You need to understand why you come to the office and what gives you personal satisfaction. Most of all, you need to understand what fuels your passion.

I have found that that the Simple Truth philosophy builds self-esteem not only in my employees but in me as well. Going down the Simple Truth path has been one of the greatest gifts I have ever given myself, an unintended consequence.

The Simple Truth process gave me peacefulness and calm in relating to my people and in looking at the future. Sure, I still have the inevitable daily crises inherent to owning a business, but I'm much better able to deal with them.

I used to have to fight for any progress I wanted to make. I may not have been the smartest person in the room, but I was always the most committed. I'd muscle my way forward, never letting the odds deter me from my destination.

As I have seen the Simple Truth work, I realize it has taken up much of the load I used to carry. I am not in this alone. I appreciate more than ever those who live it with me.

The clarity of knowing how to proceed, how to make decisions, and how to deliver on promises releases people to do what they want to do, not just what they need to do. I don't have to do it all, nor do I have to be there every moment to make sure it gets done right.

Recently, one of my competitors told me that he did not understand how I could be so graceful in this hard business. At first I was taken aback. Then I realized that I would have made the same comment had I been sitting in his chair, running my business the way I did before I discovered the Simple Truth.

This quiet confidence rubs off on people, and often I believe it is the single greatest gift I have received on this journey. Totally unintended, but totally appreciated.

The journey to the Simple Truth begins with finding clarity — clarity in how the customer sees your product or service. Businesses often talk about the customer's perspective, but they seldom achieve it. You must be totally committed to accepting the good and bad of what you may find.

The Search

"Research is what I do when I don't know what I'm doing."
— ALBERT EINSTEIN

AS WOULD BE EXPECTED, DISCOVERING YOUR SIMPLE TRUTH requires you to assess your business. Simply put, you ask your customers and employees about their needs and try to understand their perspective.

But the assessment isn't really the point. Every business fad I ever embraced began with an assessment. I assessed my people, my processes, my vendors, my telephone system, and I assessed my assessment. While that all sounds fine and dandy, it ended up being only that — an assessment.

Those perfunctory assessments allowed me to hide from the true objective, to achieve understanding. Understanding is much deeper than hearing, observing, seeing, or assessing.

To achieve understanding, you must be willing to listen for what was meant and not meant, not what was said. You must be willing to understand why and not be satisfied with how. You must be willing to take off the filters and look through a magnifying glass.

How You Ask

"It is better to know some of the questions than all of the answers."
— JAMES THURBER

TO ASK THE RIGHT QUESTION, YOU MUST UNDERSTAND what you want to know as well as what you don't want to know. Interviewing people can be treacherous, and without sufficient forethought and planning, you are destined to get the wrong answers.

When I get home at the end of the day, I love to play with my daughters. Lexie is a precocious pre-schooler, and Addie is a very active second grader. Like any interested parent, I want to know how Addie's day went at school. So I used to ask her, "Addie, how was school today?"

Her answer was basically the same every day, "Oh, okay."

It took me about a month to realize that I was asking what I wanted to know, not what she wanted to tell me. Now I ask, "Addie, what was the best thing that happened to you at school today?" Or to keep her from catching on, I'll ask, "Addie, what was the worst part of school today?"

The change has been amazing. If I can get her to engage long enough to answer my first question, she opens up and actually tells me about her day.

It's not that different from talking to customers. When a customer replies "fine" to "How was your meal?" we know that we asked the wrong question, even though we literally wanted to know how she enjoyed the meal.

When a customer says "fine," she sends a strong signal that she doesn't want to risk telling you what you may not want to hear. Most people avoid confrontation, especially with those to whom they do not have a strong connection. "Fine" is more than a cop-out on the customer's part; it is a signal that you may not have a strong relationship with that customer. And without a strong relationship, customers can be lost in the slightest break-down in meeting expectations.

Also, let me make it clear that conducting an assessment or "understanding" is not a one-time event. It is an ongoing way of life. Asking questions has two benefits. First, it lets customers or employees know that you care, and that they are important to you. Second, it allows you to be in synch with any changes in your customers' needs. It is important to run at your customer's speed — not too far ahead and not too far behind.

One of our best lunch customers comes to Brennan's of Houston four or five times per month to entertain clients for his commercial printing business. We always seat him at the same table and we know exactly what he wants. Our relationship is all about helping him do business by making business memories.

One day, sounding aggravated, he said that he had not come the previous week because he couldn't seem to get anybody at our restaurant to answer the phone. We require reservations, and with no one answering, he couldn't make one.

We had been stuck in an "it's not our fault; it's theirs" battle between our service provider and Southwestern Bell which owns the lines. Sometimes when a call came in, it would not fall into our automated attendant system, which meant that it would not be answered even though the caller heard a ring. Our customers thought we simply weren't answering the phone.

My right hand, Kathryne Castellanos, immediately explained what had happened, and he accepted her apology. But the incident made us think. First, how many other customers had we lost or disappointed because we had no alternate way to communicate? Second, we remembered that we'd been dealing with our new Internet project just the day before. That was one answer to our problem. If our customers could make reservations on-line, they wouldn't be as frustrated by a problem with our phones. And if we could e-mail our customers, we could alert them to any event that might affect our relationship.

Naturally, the online system became a higher priority, not because it's sexy and high-tech, but because it meets our customers' needs.

And it worked. The customer who alerted us to the problem was so pleased, he's been telling other customers about the web site.

What You Want to Know

"The Good Lord gave us two eyes, two ears and one mouth.
I believe he intended for us to use them in that proportion."

— UNKNOWN

BEFORE YOU START ASKING QUESTIONS, BE SURE YOU KNOW exactly what you are looking for. To understand your business, you must understand four things:

- ☞ **The Simple Truth** — what uniquely defines your business from the customer's perspective.
- ☞ **Hurdles** — the barriers that the customer must cross to do business with you, and employees must cross to work for you.
- ☞ **Secret Ingredient** – that extra element that sets you apart.
- ☞ **Your Lagniappe** — the unexpected little something that cements you in your customer's heart.

Understanding why a customer crosses hurdles allows you to understand why your product is sought after or preferred. The Secret Ingredient is the signature that your business will be known for. The all-important combination of the Simple Truth and the Secret Ingredient differentiates your product or service and provides value to your brand identity. And the lagniappe goes the extra step to guarantee your customer's brand loyalty.

Your Business's Simple Truth

"Everything should be made as simple as possible, but not one bit simpler."
— ALBERT EINSTEIN

HOW YOU DEFINE YOUR BUSINESS IS EXTREMELY IMPORTANT because it defines how you see yourself and how you approach the business. If I defined my business as serving food or operating a restaurant, I could sell the same seafood platters as Red Lobster and the same steaks as Ryan's Steak House and still work within my definition.

I felt I needed more focus, so a week after The Big Meeting I called my staff together and apologized that I, as their leader, had forgotten the basic tenet of customer service. I challenged each of them to visit with their best customers and other staff members and to bring what they learned to the next staff meeting.

At that next meeting, I listened intently to their reports, then led the group in brainstorming about what our product really is as seen from the customer's perspective. It was a how-high-is-up gathering. Everyone sensed we were onto something important.

When we tried to describe what our customers are really buying, we began with all the expected answers: great food, superior service, the prestige of the Brennan's name, and a New Orleans atmosphere.

But one of the dining room managers pointed toward something different. "The Waldrops kept talking about all the memories they have and about their great nights at Brennan's of Houston," he said. "And if it's a special time in their lives, this is the place they want to commemorate it. They can get a gourmet meal at a lot of places, but they can't get what they get here."

That comment resonated with me. I thought back on all the guest experiences I've witnessed during the last thirty years. I recalled that the guests with the biggest smiles were the ones who came for a special occasion. I decided to explore the "memories" concept with other customers.

One long-time patron told me the reason he came to our restaurants had little to do with the food. "I come here because I can celebrate with friends and know it will be an unforgettable evening," he said. "It's not about food, Alex. It's about experiences."

That was it! I felt as if my pastry chef had thrown a pecan pie in my face. I was not only shocked but also a little embarrassed that I hadn't seen my business from the customer's perspective.

I continued to ask customers how they saw the experience we delivered. They all spoke of our service, food specialties that we are known for, as well as our ambiance and food reputation. But in addition, they all expressed the same sentiment: They wanted the occasion to be memorable.

Not every customer used the word "memories." Certainly most customers come for a gourmet experience or to ensure that their guests have a wonderful time. But my most valued long-term customers all used some variation of the "memories" theme to describe why they returned year after year, gladly jumping the hurdles in their paths.

I mulled these observations. During my period of reflection, I worked on the new Commander's Palace we were opening in Las Vegas. On Thanksgiving morning as I tried to get from my hotel to the new restaurant, I found myself stuck in foot traffic on Las Vegas Blvd. I was irritated.

People were risking life and limb by stopping traffic so they could take photos. Just then, I understood the reason people own cameras and spend money to develop and display pictures. They want a memory! They want the experience to last.

My customers were willing to cross the hurdles to get to my restaurant just as these tourists were willing to risk their lives to take a photograph. That's how powerful memories can be!

At our next senior staff meeting, I told my team the Las Vegas story. "Gang," I said, "I think we're all about memories. Not food." I said it without much conviction because I wanted to see their reaction to the idea, not to my ability to sell the idea.

Their eyes lit up, and smiles crossed their faces. The group picked up where I left off and began discussing the concept of memories. They each had heard similar terms from the customers they interviewed, but no one had put it as simply as I had.

"I agree we're about customer memories," said one of the managers, "but I think we should be about great customer memories. We want to be a great restaurant and a great place to work, so we need to create great memories to achieve our goals."

We all agreed.

Our Simple Truth is "Creating Great Customer Memories."

I did not have to act like Moses coming down from the mountaintop with stone tablets. I had put the idea on the table, but the team took it from there. It had become their idea, not mine.

"Great customer memories" has not only become the definition of our product, but the phrase that keeps us on track when the pressure of instant response to customer demands could divert our focus. Every member of our restaurants teams simply stops for a second and asks himself or herself, "Does that decision help make a great memory for my customer?"

We spend a lot of time helping our people understand what makes great customer memories. Every person, from the reservationist to the dishwasher to the chef, knows that all of Brennan's employees are supporting the same product defined by the same standard of excellence — the customer's.

The rule is easy for our people to understand. If something creates a great customer memory, do it. If it doesn't, don't do it. A complex strategy becomes simple to execute.

Hurdles

*"It cannot be too often repeated that it is not helps,
but obstacles, not facilities, but difficulties that make men."*
—WILLIAM MATTHEWS

THE JOURNEY OF FINDING YOUR SIMPLE TRUTH BEGINS WITH defining and understanding the hurdles that make it harder for a customer to do business with you. As strange as it sounds, I have found hurdles to be the test of customer and employee loyalty and satisfaction.

CUSTOMER HURDLES

"Every difficulty slurred over will be a ghost to disturb your repose later on."
— FREDRIC CHOPIN

Your hurdles will be different, but here are the main hurdles our customers face at Brennan's of Houston:

☞ **$60 per person average check for dinner**
Let's be honest. We buy much of our fish from the same supplier as most other top restaurants in town. (The same can be said about our produce, ingredients, and wines.) But our strategy is to be priced at the mid-level of the high-end restaurants. We are not the most expensive restaurant, but we are a long way from Red Lobster. We ask

our customers to pay $25 for a fish entrée when they can get basically the same piece of fish for $12 at other restaurants in the neighborhood.

☞ Jacket required

As a high-end restaurant, and as a manifestation of our Southern hospitality style of service, we ask in the evening that gentlemen wear jackets. (Most of our customers even believe we require ties!) With the trend to casual dressing, this requirement became a major hurdle, but we feel it adds to the experience. When you spend $240 for a dinner for four, you don't want to be seated in a dining room with people in T-shirts and shorts.

☞ Access

Although our restaurant is located in car-loving Houston, we lack the usual large parking lot. Valet parking is the only way we can handle the cars for the large number of customers we attract. So add another five bucks to the cost of dining with us, and then expect to wait in the Houston heat and humidity while we bring your car to you.

☞ Convenience

Brennan's of Houston isn't located in a residential area, so it must draw customers from all over the city and surrounding areas. On a customer's journey to Brennan's of Houston, he could easily pass as many as 100 other restaurants.

☞ Reservations

Brennan's of Houston requires reservations because we want to ensure that a customer's table is ready for that big meeting or celebration. Most restaurants don't require customers to anticipate when they'll be hungry.

EMPLOYEE HURDLES

"Difficulties exist to be surmounted."

— RALPH WALDO EMERSON

Our employees cross hurdles to get to work every day. We have
defined four major ones:

☞ **Transportation**

Houston has a poor mass transit system, and many of our
employees do not own cars. They have to make an extra
effort to arrive at the restaurant on time.

☞ **High standards**

We demand employees' best and that they hold each other
accountable to a high standard. What may be good enough
at other restaurants won't cut it at our place. For the same
wages, our employees could work less and still be considered
stars at most restaurants in town.

Many places urge employees to go beyond the call
of duty to meet customer needs or help a fellow
employee. There is no "beyond the call of duty" at
Brennan's of Houston; that is a minimum performance
expectation. You are also expected to not only do
your job, but to help anyone who needs a hand with
his or her job.

☞ **Low wages**

Sadly, restaurants jobs are not high-paying, especially in
the service support and some kitchen areas. The restaurant
business makes a great career and provides a nice living for

a lot of people, but it is not one in which most workers grow rich.

☞ Low status

The last barrier is a pet peeve of mine. We ask our people to work weekends, nights and holidays when their friends and family members are not at work. Then many customers treat them like menial servants. Adding insult to injury, in this country we continue to use tips to compensate them for their efforts. It's somewhat demeaning to depend on tips as the primary source of income. After all, we don't tip salesmen, retail clerks, accountants or nurses.

Identifying the hurdles has two benefits. First, it forces you to understand your business, take off the "rightness" filters, and admit you have problems. But you don't have to be perfect to satisfy customers.

Second, the hurdles show you where you're most vulnerable. That knowledge allows you to defend yourself and find a way to make it up to your customers.

When you understand your the hurdles, you are on your way to finding your Simple Truth.

Your Secret Ingredient

"The secret of business is to know something that nobody else knows."
— ARISTOTLE ONASSIS

AT OUR RESTAURANTS, OUR SIMPLE TRUTH, "MAKING GREAT customer memories," cannot stand alone. We must create a unique environment for the memory to come to life. We call it our Secret Ingredient.

How, you ask, does the Simple Truth differ from the Secret Ingredient? Actually, the two need to be so tightly integrated that it is often difficult to separate them.

The Secret Ingredient is that part of the experience that connects the customer to the Simple Truth. Customers come to you to get the Simple Truth; they come back because of the Secret Ingredient.

From a branding standpoint, the Secret Ingredient becomes your signature or brand identity. It determines how people feel after they have done business with you.

The Secret Ingredient has everything to do with how your people behave and deliver a product in a superior way. It's the intangible that makes customers want to continue to do business with you. It's something that happens between people. Successful organizations understand the importance of their Secret Ingredients, and they reward employees who make individual, human connections with their customers.

At our restaurants our Secret Ingredient is "Southern hospitality," a timeworn phrase, but one that holds special meaning to us. Southern hospitality, as my mother told me when I was growing up, is the art of making your guests feel at home, even though you wish they were.

For those of us raised in the South, hospitality is as vital to our being as bourbon to a mint julep. It's more than good manners; it's an attitude that we all believe in and respect. It's the soul of our pride. It can't be forced, and it can't be faked, but it can be learned.

At Brennan's of Houston, Southern hospitality is like the spice in a great dish. It gives our restaurant character.

Are there other restaurants in Houston with a Southern heritage? Sure. But does Southern hospitality inoculate those restaurants' employees against customers they wish would go home? No!

The most recent edition of the Houston-area Zagat Survey of restaurants ranked Brennan's as the second-most popular restaurant in Houston, ahead of many newer and hipper places. Why would a restaurant that has been around for 35 years and puts such high hurdles in front of its customers be ranked so high?

Part of the answer lies in the service ranking. These comments appeared in the Zagat:

"Just about as close to perfection as you can get."
"This stalwart exemplifies Southern charm."
"Sophisticated-yet-friendly service and wonderful atmosphere."
"Ideal for special occasions and wowing out-of-towners."

My favorite quote came from one of the survey respondents. "Even New Orleans doesn't have a better New Orleans restaurant than Brennan's of Houston." Here's what Southern hospitality looks like at Brennan's of Houston:

☞ Our staff acts like human beings, not robots. They're encouraged to show their individual personalities and have fun with the customers. Instead of following a script, they make one-on-one human connections with the guests they're serving.

Usually, those guests want to have a good time. "Play if the customer is in a mood to play," my mom says. And she's right. Playing is a great way to make a memory.

☞ We address the hosts and long-term customers by their honorific and surname (Ms. X, Dr. Y) during every interaction. We welcome them warmly on arrival and show that we remember who they are and what they like. We try to show that to us, they're not the Party of Four at Table Eight. They're friends.

☞ Our staff does not use carts to clear dishes from the table; they carry them in their arms or on trays. Carts are used in factories, not in homes.

☞ We use a service style referred to as "gang service." Depending on the size of the dining party, at least two waiters will approach the table at the same time and stand behind those seated at the table. In synchrony, the two waiters will place two entrées on the table. They do so with a little flair and ceremony to make the experience extra special.

☞ We make our goodbye as warm as our hello. Even after our customers have paid the check, we make it clear that we care. As they're leaving, we thank them warmly and give them a lagniappe, a little gift of our pecan pralines (more on those later).

The combination of the Simple Truth and a Magic Ingredient makes a business unique — and that uniqueness directly affects the business's bottom line. In the case of our restaurants, it affects our prices.

RESOURCES

Galveston, TX 77551

August 31, 1996

Brennan's
3300 Smith Street
Houston, Texas 77066

Dear Mr. Brennan-Martin;

Several weeks ago my business partner and I had lunch with a client at your restaurant. I was dressed in clothing appropriate to be in a just- moved- into- art - studio, not for dining at Brennan's. Your staff very graciously allowed me in. I have not been so well taken care of in a restaurant, even when "dressed to the nines." The person who took such wonderful care of us was Paul Parker. I have dined in many restaurants in my life, but this experience will always stand out. Mr. Parker was warm and friendly and caught the mood of our meeting, which was partly a celebration of our clients new work in life as an artist. I want to acknowledge Mr. Parker for not only serving wonderful food and drink to us in a very gracious manner, but for joining are play and teasing and adding to the celebration. It is a pleasure to write an acknowledgement, especially when this week I have had to write two letters on behalf of clients who are not being treated properly by other business establishments.

I look forward to dining at Brennan's again, and will let others know of the wonderful food, atmosphere and staff that are there.

Sincerely,

insights that impact

Prices and the Secret Ingredient

"A nickel ain't worth a dime anymore."
— YOGI BERRA

IF ALL WE WERE SELLING AT BRENNAN'S OF HOUSTON IS sautéed fish, we would have to compete on price. But since we are selling great memories, price is only one component of the value equation.

A common misunderstanding is that an item should be priced as low as possible to attract more customers and create the potential for a higher volume. In many cases that may be true, but not every time.

Experience has taught me that price matters more than anything else only when you allow it to and only when you allow your products and services to become commodities.

The role of price is to get your business in the "considered set." That means you have to price your products in a range that the customer will consider paying.

For example, Starbucks sells a cup of coffee for $3.00. Some coffee shops sell virtually the same coffee for $1.25. But if you tried to charge $5.00 for a cup, no one in his right mind would consider buying it. So no matter how much value you add, there is a limit to what the customer will pay.

The obvious question is this: How can our restaurants charge $3 for iced tea while another restaurant charges only $1.75? We buy our tea from the same supplier, our water comes from the same city system, and for the most part, we pay about the same rates to our wait staff.

But we serve the tea in a fine glass and use top-of-the-line flatware. We seat our customers in a comfortable chair at a table with a starched white tablecloth and candle. We surround them with New Orleans atmosphere and serve the finest in Southern hospitality. In other words, we add our Secret Ingredient to the tea.

One last comment about the role of price: Price gets you considered, but it does not build a relationship. Relationships are about people connecting through shared experiences, not about how much something costs.

Price is the rational part of the value equation. Service and the experience are the emotional elements. And it is the emotional elements that form the basis of a relationship and create the great memories.

A remarkable grocery store chain demonstrated how powerful the emotional and relationship aspects of price are to the customer. In its prime, Randall's dominated the Houston market (the chain was sold to Safeway a few years ago). It was known for its service and developed a reputation as the silk-stocking store.

As would be expected, Randall's prices were slightly higher than many of the other large grocery stores. But only marginally higher.

I once heard about research that showed that Randall's prices were actually lower than the prices the customers thought they were paying. In other words, Randall's was leaving money on the table because its customer were so willing to pay a premium to have a relationship, they just assumed they were paying higher prices.

We have always tried to be priced in the mid-range of our competitive group. We choose to leave the extra money on the table to enhance the memory of the customer while striving to be better than our competitors. That value perception builds slowly over time, but it does build, and it becomes another competitive advantage.

The following letter from one of our valued customers that demonstrates the role of price in the Brennan's of Houston great-memories experience:

STEWART & STEVENSON
CORPORATE HEADQUARTERS

March 16, 2000

Brennan's
3300 Smith Street
Houston, Texas 77002

Attention: Ellen Tipton and Lydia Perez

Ref: Stewart/Johnson Rehearsal Dinner – October 22, 1999

Dear Ellen and Lydia,

I apologize for the delay in writing you with regard to our son Rob and Kristi's rehearsal dinner that we held in the upstairs ballroom on the evening of October 22, 1999. The entire event went flawlessly and the food was absolutely superb! It was truly a memorable evening for the entire 104 guests we had in attendance. Brennan's truly lived up to its long-standing reputation of having the highest level of quality and elegance. There was not one thing that my wife or I felt could have, or should have gone differently during the entire evening. Your entire staff was professional and made the dinner one that will be forever remembered.

The truly unique thing is that I sincerely feel that the value that we received for this incredibly wonderful evening was most fair. This may seem a little unusual for someone to write to you about, but I felt it was my obligation to do this after having hosted another rehearsal dinner on March 3, 2000 at ███████████ for my other son and his fiancée. Whereas the food was all right and the service satisfactory, we were billed in excess of $5,000 more for virtually the same number of guests. The cost difference on a per guest basis was $41.25. ███████████ charged $131.72 per guest (110) and Brennan's was $90.48 per guest (104). This represents over 45% more for virtually the same exact type program. I sincerely believe that Brennan's, with its long and outstanding history and reputation is in this business for the long term as opposed to others. You must always maintain certain key elements in doing business anywhere and that is fairness and integrity, which will develop a loyal client base. We will be back time and time again!

Sincerely,

C. Jim Stewart III
Vice President

63

Your Lagniappe

"We picked up one excellent word — a word worth traveling to New Orleans to get; a nice, limber, expressive handy word — 'Lagniappe.'"
— MARK TWAIN

THERE IS ONE OTHER IMPORTANT ELEMENT IN SOUTHERN hospitality that we practice at our restaurants. We use the Creole word "lagniappe" (pronounced "lah-nyap") to mean something extra, a gift or token of appreciation. No New Orleans hostess would let her guests leave without a little lagniappe.

The power of the lagniappe is that it appears after the customer thinks the experience is over. Because it's unexpected, the little extra has much more power.

By the doorway of Brennan's of Houston, a silver platter is always stacked high with our famous homemade pecan pralines. Customers are encouraged to help themselves to one or two on the way out. And if they're too full, or want to take a little something home to a family member, we even put the pralines in a specially-designed Brennan's of Houston bag.

We spend thousands of dollars a year giving away a trademark product that could be a significant revenue source. We give it away because nothing else better exemplifies Southern hospitality, and because it is the perfect way to anchor a great memory as the customer walks out the door.

In developing your own personal lagniappe, try to make it

relevant to your Simple Truth and Secret Ingredient. That way, the little gift packs a greater wallop. Your lagniappe might be throwing in an extra tie when a customer buys several suits, or a baker's dozen for the price of a regular dozen, or a funny song on the public address system when the plane lands.

It's not the cost of the lagniappe, but the act of offering it that sends the message. You are a welcomed friend, please come back.

PERSONAL LAGNIAPPE

"Criticism has the power to do good when there is something that must be destroyed, dissolved, or reduced, but it is capable only of harm when there is something to be built."
— CARL JUNG

I also believe in the personal lagniappe. It is the extra smile or pat on the back to those you work with. It is taking the time to connect with the guest in a personal way. These little actions may seem inconsequential in today's fast-paced world, but that's just the point. Small gestures are big gifts, and people remember them.

They're also a gift that helps the giver. Knowing that I've made a difference spurs me on. And as my young managers grow into their roles, I enjoy seeing them get the lift of giving a little extra to someone who didn't expect it.

You can't put on an act. You've got to really mean it. Woody Allen says that 90 percent of life is showing up, and we all know lots of employees who just show up. But when one gives that extra ten percent, it makes all the difference in the world to your business. Once you realize that, honestly showing your appreciation is easy.

COMMUNITY LAGNIAPPE

"We make a living by what we get, we make a life by what we give."

— WINSTON CHURCHILL

My family also taught me about community lagniappe — giving back to the community as thanks for its support and friendship. Sure, it's good for our business to serve on the board of non-profit organizations and give time, money and food to community causes. But more important, being involved until it hurts makes us feel more connected to the community.

For fundraising and charity events, we often provide our famous turtle soup. ("The Turtle Soup Show," my staff calls it.) By giving away our signature soup, we're not only helping a good cause. We're giving people a taste of what makes us special.

Those events also build pride in our people. They come back with stories about customers they've seen and are proud to be part of the Brennan's of Houston family not only because of what we do, but even more because of who we are. We're the kind of people who give back to the community.

Delivering
the Simple Truth

"There are two ways of spreading light:
to be the candle or the mirror that reflects it."
— EDITH WHARTON

LONG AGO SOMEONE ASKED MY MOTHER, ELLA BRENNAN, HOW she'd built her remarkably strong repeat clientele. "First," she said, "make a friend."

You look a friend in the eye and smile. When your friends come to your home for dinner, you straighten up the place. You put on your good clothes, not to impress your friends, but to show respect for them.

We do the same at Brennan's of Houston. Here's a passage from our orientation manual:

The first step in our process is to make our guests feel comfortable from the moment they arrive. We do that by words and body language. Walking into a fine dining restaurant can be intimidating for some people. We want to surprise them with a heart-felt greeting instead of a half-hearted hello. I believe people don't get welcomed warmly often enough in today's world. If we go out of our way to say "welcome" and "smile" with your whole body, we have almost won the battle the first time we engage the customer. These greetings must be sincere, and you have to truly mean it. You can't fake people on this one.

The next step is to connect with each person in the party. Too often people have to settle for feeling like a cog in a machine, like they are being churned out and perfunctorily told they are important. Our customers give us clues as to why they are here. Look at the information they are giving you, or simply engage them in a bit of conversation, and they will tell you what you need to know.

My favorite technique is a question that I ask at the beginning of service: "Are you on a schedule this evening, or can you take your time and relax a bit tonight?" Right off the bat you will know how the meal should go: quickly to get them to a play or other event on time, or slowly, knowing they will not be frustrated by a leisurely service pace. It also puts the customer at ease, knowing from the very beginning that you are going to tailor the experience to his or her specific desires. Servers can relay this information to the kitchen and managers to make sure everything moves at the speed of the customer.

Eye contact is extremely valuable. Search out the customer's eyes at every occasion, and he or she will signal his or her desires. This is perhaps the most missed opportunity to make a connection, and it is the easiest to correct. Make it a practice to never leave a station or encounter with a guest without looking the customer directly in the eye. It is the best way I have found to work smarter rather than harder, and to make genuine human contact with a customer.

The final method is to follow through all the way, not ever settling for good enough. Good enough is not a pride-building practice. You've done the hard work of getting dressed, traveling to work, and doing the mechanics of your job. Now, follow through and give it your best, and you will feel your best. And feeling your best is key to giving the customer a great memory.

Creating great customer memories may be hard to define, but you know it when you see it. It is using our reservation system to keep profiles of our regular customers, and preparing ahead of time for their particular needs. It is being close at hand after the check is presented so you can answer any questions. It is a warm goodbye and thanking the customers for the opportunity to serve them.

It is asking them to come back to our "home" soon.

Staying On Track

"Even if you're on the right track, you'll get run over if you just sit there."
— WILL ROGERS

TO VISUALIZE THE PERFECT ALIGNMENT BETWEEN A CUSTOMER and employee, imagine a railroad track. When the customer and employee's needs are aligned, they become parallel, like a railroad track. The ties that hold the tracks together are the small steps, one after another, that connect the employee to the customer all the way to the end of the line. On a strongly built railroad track, a business relationship can move forward no matter the terrain or weather.

Our team passed through rough weather and bumpy terrain when we opened Commander's Palace in Las Vegas. We refer to the experience as the "Perfect Storm." To mix transportation metaphors: Had we not been "railroading," our ship would have sunk.

I was excited about opening Commander's Palace in Las Vegas. Many of our Houston and New Orleans customers went to Las Vegas regularly, and though gaming might be the main attraction, many of the best "in" restaurants in America had opened there.

My family's group, the Commander's Palace Family of Restaurants, was exploring ways to expand our business, so we researched Las Vegas. We found what appeared to be the perfect opportunity. (Beware of perfect opportunities!)

The old Aladdin Hotel on Las Vegas Blvd., in the heart of the Vegas strip, was being renovated, and the owners were looking for a big-name restaurant as a tenant. We decided to roll the dice.

The night after we signed the lease, I woke up in a cold sweat. I had just agreed to be a partner in opening only the second Commander's Palace in 128 years. Many of the New Orleans customers would dine at the Las Vegas restaurant. They would be more familiar with the Commander's style of service and dining experience than the hundred or so new employees who would deliver the Commander's experience to the customers.

From the start, Commander's Palace Las Vegas ran into trouble. During construction, we had countless conflicts with the landlord and hotel; some seriously threatened the project's viability. At the same time, the opening of the new Aladdin was a disaster, and during its first year of operation, things only grew worse.

Our perfect storm came within months of the restaurant's opening. In Vegas fashion, we were thrown two elevens: The September 11 disaster occurred within weeks of the Aladdin's filing Chapter 11. Most of the mall's original tenants and the hotel restaurants closed shortly thereafter.

The press and buzz about the hotel and mall could not have been worse. Because of the Chapter 11 filing, many people believed the entire complex was closed, including our restaurant.

We could have become distracted or even despondent , but railroading kept employees focused on what mattered, the customers that we did have. Led by my cousin Brad Brennan, our team stuck to the Simple Truth.

We played the cards we were dealt and managed to win the hand. As Larry said in his introduction to the book, our customers have returned time and again. The readers of *Las Vegas Life Magazine* voted Commander's Palace Las Vegas the city's best new restaurant, and a year later, the best restaurant on the Las Vegas Strip! Even more astounding, many of our customers say they prefer the Las Vegas Commander's Palace to the one in New Orleans.

Asking Customers

"Quality is never an accident; it is always the result of intelligent efforts."
— JOHN RUSKIN

ONE OF THE BEST TECHNIQUES TO STAY ON TRACK SOUNDS easy but is difficult to do well. Talk to the customer. At our restaurants, we aim to talk with our customers in ways that add to their great memories rather than interfere with their dining experiences.

We have refined what we need to know to a very short list of questions. The simpler we make the process, the more often we use it, and the easier it is to stay focused on what's important.

The following are the basic things we want to know from our customers' perspective:

- What makes our restaurants different from other places you dine?
- Do you feel we made personal contact during your dining experience?
- Was anything difficult about doing business with us?
- What stands out for you about your experience with us?
- How satisfied are you with the value of your meal, and do you feel you got your money's worth?
- What do you tell your friends about your experiences dining with us?

Of course, many customers don't like to talk. But the non-talkers' opinions are important too, so we developed a feedback system that gives us the information we need without making them feel uncomfortable.

In our early years we used self-addressed and stamped cards so that folks could communicate to us on their own schedules and without having to experience any potential discomfort. The customer-comment cards worked well — we received both positive and negative comments, and actually got a good number of our guests to respond — but we've since found better methods.

In 1995 we put a voice mailbox number on the comment cards. The number of comments from customers increased significantly because it was easier for many customers to call rather than to write. Interestingly, many of our customers called on the way home from our restaurant.

Now we are using the Internet to connect with our customers. We steer people to our web site where there is a "How are we doing?" button. (I stole the question from former New York Mayor Ed Koch.)

Through e-mail we receive three to four times more comments than before, and we find them to be more thoughtful and specific. E-mail also allows us to respond to each person, showing that we care. It strengthens our relationship to the customer.

Dear Mr. Brennan-Martin:

I am compelled to write you to let you know of a special experience my wife, Jan, and I had at your restaurant last night. From the time we arrived and were greeted warmly by Kathryne Castellanos, were waited on superbly by Thomas and served with panache by Chefs Chris and Randy, until we departed some two hours later, we were treated as if we were celebrities, with care and warmth. It was an experience we'll never forget. As always, the food and wines were superlative and the setting and ambiance delightful.

We've been coming to Brennan's since 1974, when we first moved to Houston. We've been there for dinners, lunches, (many times at the monthly West Point Society luncheon that Pino directs so well), for brunches that are always memorable, and for Christmas parties put on by Steve and Nancy Martin (also ably directed by Pino). We enjoyed New Year's Eve dinner there last year and plan to make it and annual affair. Most recently, I enjoyed a cooking class on Father's Day eve, compliments of my four children and was delighted to meet Chefs Carl and Chris and Randy and Kathryne.

Every time I've been there has been better than the last time. I've been to restaurants, fine and otherwise, all over the world including in London and Paris and Rome but Brennan's is, and will always be, my favorite. Not only have I always has a great meal, I've experienced one of the best aspects of life that only a combination of good food, good wine and joy in its creation and serving, and, most important of all, in it pleasurable consumption canbring.

I thank you and all the staff and wish you continuing success.

Sincerely,
Robert F. La Raia

DANIEL G. DUKE, M.D.

OPHTHALMOLOGY AND OPHTHALMIC SURGERY

8601 VILLAGE DRIVE

SUITE 212

SAN ANTONIO, TEXAS 78217

(210) 656-3533

FAX (210) 656-4493

E-MAIL dduke101@aol.com

DIPLOMATE OF THE AMERICAN
BOARD OF OPHTHALMOLOGY

April 22, 2002

Brennan's of Houston
3300 Smith Street
Houston, TX 77006-9711

Dear Ladies and Gentlemen:

In 1973, I came to Houston to meet old high school friends, and to take the licensing exam of the Texas State Board of Medical Examiners. We chose that weekend to dine at Brennan's. We all had little money, but felt the experience was worth every penny.

Last Saturday night, I joined one of those old friends, almost thirty years later, for dinner again at your restaurant. He and I have changed in many ways. Brennan's has not. Only the patina of a mature operation catches the eye. From the aroma of garlic suffusing the air as one walks in the door, to the romantically lit room, to the incomparably correct service, to the heavenly food and wine, I just love it. Life is just too short. But while I am here, the pleasures of the table at Brennan's will remain on my calendar.

Just want you to know you are appreciated.

Sincerely yours,

Daniel G. Duke, M. D.

DGD:ld

To: All Employees of Brennan's of Houston
From: Alex Brennan-Martin
Date: 4/27/02
Re: A letter from a longtime customer

Every so often one of our customers does us the great favor of sitting down and writing us a letter of complaint detailing how from his perspective we failed to deliver "the memory" he was expecting from us. I value these letters because while it is never fun hearing how badly we have done from one of our customers it is truly a lesson with "customer eyes". It comes from this perspective not ours and is so invaluable.

We share these with you from time to time so that we can all learn and profit from them. They point out areas in which we can improve and sometimes point out larger problems that demand swift action and change of systems or worse.

Many of you have seen those kinds of letters or heard those kinds of comments we have received from customers. You know how we focus on them and that our policy of "overwhelming response" might well mean you get to go on a "prize patrol". We use these opportunities to get better; it's the "process of continual improvement", which is the first thing we talk to you about in our philosophy orientation and manual. We truly understand the value of these moments.

Most of you have also seen letters of praise as well; we post them on the bulletin board by the time clock and pass them on to all involved. I think sometimes we don't do enough with them compared with more negative feedback.

That's just as big a mistake as not focusing on customer complaints.

The letter I am attaching made me realize this. Rarely, if ever, in my career have I received a letter or comment that spans almost the entire life span of our restaurant. Please notice it is addressed not to me but to "Dear Ladies and Gentlemen". This letter is for all of us so I wanted to share it with you and tell you again how proud I am of each of you.

What you do matters!

This customer has had great memories of us for almost thirty years and on his recent return visit we did it again! We didn't let him down; in fact we did so well we moved him to write this extraordinary letter. If that doesn't light your fire well then your wood's wet!

This is why I am in this business and I hope it is why you are as well. Allow yourself a moment to realize just how important we are to this gentleman then look at your next table or tray going out and realize we are truly in "the memory making business" and that's the opportunity right in front of you right now. We are lucky to be in this business!

Congratulations and enjoy the letter!

Fortunately we now receive more positive comments than ever before. The comments are passed along to all the employees involved, so they receive the reward of being thanked by a guest. And we can see evidence that the Simple Truth is working.

Asking Employees

"Many receive advice. Only the wise profit by it."
— PUBLILIUS SYRUS

AS I SAID EARLIER, THE CUSTOMER IS NOT THE ONLY COMMU-
nity vital to our business's success. Though I emphasize talking to
customers, I also talk to the other key community — employees.

(The owner is the third community, but I talk to myself
enough as it is.)

There are actually two employee groups: managers and
lower-level employees. They should be approached differently.

For managers, three questions are vital. How they answer
immediately tells you whether they understand their roles in the
success of your business and whether they are living the Simple
Truth way of life:

☞ Where do you create value in the process of making great
   customer memories?
☞ What role do you play in our Simple Truth?
☞ Where do you add economic value to our business?

These questions are another way of asking where they fit into
the philosophy and what unique part they play. Like a flywheel on
a machine, they must mesh with the rest of the organization,
and there is a specific place where they get traction with the team

and the customer. Unless the managers understand how they add economic value, they don't understand your business sufficiently to manage it for you.

If they're unclear on these points, they will spend all their time putting out fires which will allow them the illusion of progress. They will be firemen rather than managers.

As for our employees, we consistently ask how they feel. We want to know:

☞ Do you feel you are being controlled at work?

☞ Is this a happy place to work?

☞ Do you feel you are learning at work and having an opportunity to grow?

☞ Are you proud to tell your friends where you work?

☞ What's the toughest part of getting to work?

☞ Do you have any close friends at work?

The Power of Plodding

" 'Slow and steady wins the race.' What's _yours_ say?"

The Tortoise and the Hare

FROM *FABLES* BY AESOP. RETOLD BY JOSEPH JACOBS

The Hare was once boasting of his speed before the other animals. "I have never yet been beaten," said he, "when I put forth my full speed. I challenge anyone here to race me."

The Tortoise said quietly, "I accept your challenge."

"That is a good joke," said the Hare: "I could dance round you all the way."

"Keep your boasting till you've beaten me," answered the Tortoise. "Shall we race?"

So a course was fixed and a start was made. The Hare darted almost out of sight at once, but soon stopped and, to show his contempt for the Tortoise, lay down to have a nap. The Tortoise plodded on and plodded on, and when the Hare awoke from his nap, he saw the Tortoise just near the winning post and could not run up in time to save the race. Then the Tortoise said:

"Plodding wins the race."

Why Focused and Steady Beats Business at the Speed of Light

"If you aim for nothing, you'll hit it every time."
— UNKNOWN

ANY DAY OR EVENING YOU WALK INTO MY RESTAURANT, YOU will probably find me wearing a tie with a turtle design. It's not because turtle soup is one of our most famous dishes (although we have sold more than 1,250,000 bowls—at Brennan's of Houston alone). The tie is to remind my people and me that, like Aesop's tortoise, we will be successful over the long course if we remain focused and steady.

The tortoise approach may seem boring in today's hare-brained, broadband world, but the moral of the story remains the same: Focused and steady wins the race. Business is a marathon, not a sprint. Sure, we must move quickly to prevent our competitors from gaining an advantage, but the real need for speed is to stay one step ahead of our customers.

Plodding is rooted in the belief that understanding and focusing on the basics of your business, combined with a predictable and steady implementation process, will allow you to be victorious over the "need for speed" methodologies heralded by business writers (who, after all, get paid to write about what's new, rather than what really works).

Warren Buffett is the role model for investment plodders. He made billions by carefully analyzing and understanding the fundamentals of businesses and not letting fads influence his investment decisions.

Buffett did not invest in the Internet because he could not understand how those companies might make a profit. And as it turns out, many of them never figured it out either.

Business at the speed of light allowed companies like Enron, WorldCom and Global Crossing to forget common sense and diverted those who should have known better from understanding the fundamentals of their businesses.

At Brennan's of Houston we don't sprint from one idea to the other, but rather, methodically develop business strategies and solutions that are always focused on the Simple Truth. We are proud to plod.

Plodders understand the difference between moving quickly and decisively and are sure they follow the customer, not the crowd. Plodders understand what's important and what's not, and stay the course when everyone else is racing like the hare.

Plodding does not mean dragging your feet or lethargically going through the motions. Rather, it is an acceptance of the powerful force of human nature and is guided by the insight that humans hate change and hate quick change even more.

Plodding, though, is a process of change. Every employee must understand that the status quo is not acceptable, nor is just knowing the right thing to do. Continual improvement is so important that it's the first concept I discuss in orientation.

Plodding means incremental and continued improvement without losing focus. We plodders pace ourselves, moving when the customer moves and never losing sight of our Simple Truth. Of course, even slow change is scary, and even plodders must take risks. One of my favorite expressions is, "Behold the turtle; he only makes progress when he sticks his neck out."

Plodding makes employees feel safe and empowers them to learn from their mistakes, not worry about dying from them.

Plodding is working with human nature, not against it.

The Core Beliefs
of Plodding

"The moment of victory is much too short to live for that and nothing else."
— MARTINA NAVRATILOVA

PLODDING IS NOT A PROCESS OR METHODOLOGY AS MUCH as it is a way of life. It is a belief system that must reside at the core of a person's business soul. This is not something you can test-drive. You have to own it before you leave the parking lot.

These are the four core beliefs of Plodding:

EVOLVE, DON'T CHANGE

Consistency requires you to be as ignorant today as you were a year ago.
—BERNARD BERENSON

This may sound like splitting hairs, but it is a major attitudinal difference. Change is an event; evolution is a process. Change is against human nature; evolution is natural.

When it's time to change something, we plodders go slowly. We hold up our Simple Truth, then challenge the proposed change to make sure its assumptions fit within our Simple Truth model. A disciplined process assures that there are no panicked reactions. It's the pace that matters most.

Viewing change as an event implies that it is an abrupt redirection of the existing process. Evolving means breaking a change into smaller pieces rather than trying to get the organization to swallow the whole thing at once.

By maintaining a singular focus on what the customer really wants and not what we think he wants, we can detect the customer's desire for a new process before it becomes a crisis. We move with the customers, and by avoiding a crisis, we can implement new procedures that are invisible to them.

A good example is light cuisine. Everyone talks about it and proclaims the health benefits of eating low-fat foods, but only a few of our guests actually choose our light offerings. Most of our customers come for a meal to remember; they want the full-bodied taste of the dish. So rather than jump on the light bandwagon, we took the time to understand what the customer was saying. What the customer wanted was smart choices and smaller portions with big taste, not a stripped-down version of a great meal.

In developing plodding processes, we live by an immutable rule: Every process begins and ends with the customer in mind. The process isn't broken until the customer begins to feel it is broken.

MAKE EVERYBODY HAPPY

"Never be haughty to the humble; never be humble to the haughty."
— JEFFERSON DAVIS

This is not some Pollyanna dream, but rather an admission that happiness is the core of a committed, motivated and loyal workforce and the basis of long-term relationships with customers.

One of my favorite country music lyrics is "When mama ain't happy, ain't nobody happy." That's the way it is at work as well. When the employees aren't happy, the customers aren't happy. When the customers aren't happy, the employees aren't happy. And when the customers and the employees aren't happy, the owner is out of business.

It is important to define happiness. It's not just the absence of unhappiness or disappointment or heartache. And it's not a giddy feeling where everyone runs around singing songs and blowing bubbles. It's an honest emotion, not some storybook concept.

We strive to achieve consistent happiness, but of course, life is filled with both ups and downs. Ignoring the downs is trying to create an artificial existence where people are expected to deny their humanness and be less authentic.

I am not a proponent of coddling people who should be fired. (More about that later.) Making everybody happy is about creating an environment where people can be productive and feel good about who they are and what they do.

MAKE THE RIGHT CHOICE

"A wise man will make more opportunities than he finds."

— SIR FRANCIS BACON

Life is about choices. When we try to make the choices for others, we take away their initiative and accountability.

At our restaurants we introduce the concept of personal choice to our staff during orientation. Rather than throw them into the job and tell them to go make good choices, we train them to use the Simple Truth as their guide.

Our message to all employees is simple and clear: To be successful, your goal should be to do the right thing in every circumstance. We make sure they understand that everyone at our restaurants is held accountable for the choices he makes. We also make it clear that if someone around you is not living up to her end of the bargain, it is not an excuse for you not to. In fact, it is an opportunity for you to shine and lead by example.

We work hard to make sure our restaurants foster that spirit in every team member. We want our employees to face these moments and seize the potential in themselves. They clearly understand that if they choose to do less or accept less in those around them, they will not do well in our restaurant — or get ahead in life.

Quite simply, it's up to each person to choose how well he or she will do. We can't and won't make their choices for them, but we will hold them accountable for what they choose.

Furthermore, we don't believe that life just happens to us or that one person is powerless to make a difference. In fact, we have seen the extraordinary change that a person can make when he or she chooses to make a difference and not succumb to the victim's mentality that plagues our world today. Being a victim is a choice.

I was fortunate to hear a great presentation by Dewitt Jones, a well-known photographer who often works for *National Geographic*. He uses his photography to talk about leadership. One of his main points was brought home to me when he made a twist on the old saying "I'll believe it when I see it."

"When I believe it," he said, "I'll see it!"

If you don't believe that you are important and can make a difference, you won't make a difference.

THE VICIOUS CYCLE VERSUS THE VIRTUOUS CYCLE

"Clear your mind of can't."
— DR. SAMUEL JOHNSON

In observing employees, I noticed that when a person made a wrong choice, it was often followed by another wrong choice, and sooner or later, by another bad choice. His sense of self took a dive. Trapped in a vicious cycle, he would spiral downward out of control.

Conversely, when a person made multiple right choices in a row, he tended to spiral upward, ascending to new heights — a "virtuous cycle."

The key to changing a Vicious Cycle into a Virtuous Cycle is coaching. "Now, how did the choice you just made fit with the Simple Truth?" I ask. That question allows me to focus on the decision-making process used for this particular problem, rather than the person's overall competence.

When I ask someone how she feels about doing something outside the Simple Truth, she usually tells me she feels bad or is mad at herself for not doing it right. I then say, "OK, you can do it again and feel really bad, or you have the choice to do it right the next time and feel good about yourself. What do you want to do? It's your choice to make."

When employees understand that they will not be fired for making one bad choice, they become more relaxed and open. When they realize that they have the power to make sure one bad choice doesn't have to become a trend, they can give themselves permission to make the right choice next time.

Making mistakes is not about being a bad person. It's about making a bad choice.

Minding Your P's And Q

"The simple virtues of willingness, readiness, alertness
and courtesy will carry a man further than mere smartness."
— RANDALL THOMAS DAVIDSON

I'M SURE THAT AS A CHILD YOUR MOTHER TOLD YOU TO MIND your P's and Q's. I never knew exactly what they were, but I got the message: Be on your best behavior, take care of business, and stay in line.

At our restaurants, we tell our people to mind their P's and Q, but we make sure they understand the importance of each letter. We have three "P's": Profit, People, and Pride. And one "Q": Quality.

Our P's and Q are all rooted in harnessing human nature, and they are the foundation of our business.

PROFIT

"Civilization and profits go hand in hand."
—CALVIN COOLIDGE

"Profit" is not a bad word. Although people always come first at our restaurants, if the business lost money, it would cease to exist. Our employees would lose their jobs, and we wouldn't be there when our customers want to make great memories. Our customers not only expect us to make a profit; they want us to, so that we'll continue to exist for them.

Our employees need to know how the business earns that profit and understand their role in doing so. They must understand how they create value and how that value aligns with our Simple Truth.

We define profit in several ways. The most obvious is return on the investment that owners expect from putting their capital at risk. The owners should receive at least a market-return rate, so they won't be tempted to put their money elsewhere.

Profit is also defined as what our people take home in their paychecks. In the restaurant busines, pay is often tied directly to how well we as a team fulfill our goal of creating great customer memories. Customer counts are either up or down, and if you are tipped, you see it in your paycheck.

I have long been frustrated by people's assumption that, as the owner of a well-known business, I must make a fortune. One evening I was standing outside the restaurant with the valets when a guest remarked, "The Ferrari parked near the front door must be Mr. Brennan's."

I couldn't resist. I introduced myself and pointed to my old Suburban parked down the street. We all had a good laugh, but that exchange made me think, "I bet my employees feel the same way."

At our next staff meeting I asked roughly 30 volunteers to come to the front of the room. I gave each of them a sign. The first sign read: "Owner." I handed him $100 in one-dollar bills. You can imagine the uproar.

I then asked the other volunteers to turn around their signs so everyone in the audience could read them. The next sign read, "Food Purveyor 27%." Others read, "Labor 25%," "Fringe Benefits 8%," and so on. The last sign listed the expenses most employees never think about, credit card fees, training, advertising, insurance, etc.

At the end of the line was a sign that read, "Owners $6." I pointed out that many of our other role-players had signs with much larger sums, and at the end of the day, the owners had only $6 of the $100 to pay them for risking their investment. Everyone else got their money first.

The feedback was rewarding. At our employee orientation, we now take everyone through a simple mathematical example to show them how we make money. Now they know that profit is not a dirty word, and that the owners are hardly the only people who enjoy the profits.

PEOPLE

"The world must learn to work together, or finally it will not work at all."
— DWIGHT D. EISENHOWER

After a long day of work, I was having a glass of wine with Brennan's of Houston's executive chef, Carl Walker. We talked about how proud we were of our people and how well they were performing. I uttered a cliché: "Carl, people are our most important asset." Carl thought for a moment, then responded: "No, Alex, people who get it are our most important asset."

Five minutes later a light bulb came on in my head. "I disagree with your earlier comment about valuable people being those who get it," I said. " The valuable people are those who live it!"

No management approach works unless people live it every day. Hiring great people and making sure they get it is just the beginning.

A sign near our water station says: "Be Nice or Leave." If employees can't be nice to each other, they won't be nice to customers. And if employees feel ill-treated, they won't want to come to work, and even if they show up, they won't have the attitude we're looking for. People who don't want to be there can infect the entire culture and create a totally unhappy place.

Being nice is the individual's responsibility. To be nice is a choice a person makes, and everyone is held accountable for his or her choices.

It may be time for a new sign in the kitchen: "Live it or leave it."

PRIDE

*"Pride is generally censured and decried,
but mainly by those who have nothing to be proud of."*
— ARTHUR SCHOPENHAUER

Pride is how someone feels, either about himself or the team he plays for. We can nurture pride, or we can take it away, but without it, the person's passion for the job quickly disappears.

Work should be a huge source of your pride. My mother always told me, "If you can't smile, stay at home." She believes that a smile is merely an outward manifestation of how you feel inside. It shows your pride.

I've taken my mother's lesson to heart. Over the employee entrance to the restaurant, I placed a large sign: "If you're not going to leave here proud, go ahead and leave now."

I like the moment in the movie *City Slickers* when slicker Billy Crystal asks wizened cowboy Jack Palance the secret to life. Palance holds up one finger. His prescription for success and happiness is to pick one thing and focus on it to the exclusion of everything else.

Here's my point: If your one thing is pride, rather than results, you stand a greater chance of delivering your Simple Truth. The natural result of Pride First is employees' willingness to do more than just their jobs.

When you lead with pride, you don't have to monitor every employee every minute of the day. You know he will do what is right by the customer because he will do what is right by him.

It's how they choose to act when you're not around that will determine your results. Who would you rather have on your team: a person motivated by pride, or a person motivated by fear of the boss?

Managers can't serve every guest, cook every plate, or clean each room. Employees do, and it's how they choose to do these tasks that determines whether or not customers return.

Here's my reality: It's not how good I am; it's how good my people are!

Sadly, our society has sunk to a point that people sometimes feel they need permission to have pride. I believe pride is a choice, and we make sure all of our people know they have the right to have pride and the responsibility to make it happen.

I begin each new employee orientation session with introductory remarks. Every time I begin with this:

> Beyond a better tip, advancement in your career or building loyal customers for the future, there is one wish I have for each of you. Quite simply, it is to develop pride in the job you've done. Having pride in what you do is the greatest opportunity to feel really good about yourself, and I always want you to feel good about who you are, not just what you do. Have you ever finished a shift and been on kind of a high? Remember that feeling, or at least try to imagine how good it would feel to know that what you did mattered. I'm tired of the overwhelming view that what we do in the restaurant industry is not important in the larger scheme of this technical world we live in.
>
> You can choose to change that! What could be more honorable than making someone happy, and giving the gift of a great memory? No, you can't put that feeling in the bank, but money can't buy that kind of self-satisfaction either. The only way you can get it is by committing to our simple goal of working for pride, and then living it every

minute from the time you walk in the door until you leave at the end of your shift.

Pride might be a corny concept today, but there is nothing corny about feeling that you matter, and that you have made a difference in the world you live in.

Pride is solely responsibility of each employee. We in management promise to deliver on our commitment and provide a good environment; the rest is up to the individual. It's just another choice you make on the road to success or failure.

I have found a very simple but powerful pride-building tool: Saying "thank you!" One of my roles as a leader is to make sure every employee knows that his or her contribution is appreciated and that his or her performance is noticed. Nothing builds pride better than hearing the boss call your name and saying "thank you."

President George Bush, George W.'s father, often frequents Brennan's of Houston. He taught me a lot about how to foster pride in employees. Even when he was the commander-in-chief, the most powerful man in the world, he took time to remember the names of many of our service staff. He even sent me a letter that I hung — proudly — in my office.

Throughout his career, and even as president, he made it a priority to send hand-written notes to people on his personal staff who performed well. He wanted them to know that he was aware and that he cared, two irreplaceable ingredients in building pride.

Building pride has become my personal Secret Ingredient.

QUALITY

"Quality isn't something that can be argued into an article or promised into it. It must be put there. If it isn't put there, the finest sales talk in the world won't act as a substitute."

— C.G. CAMPBELL

We define quality as never accepting less than the best.
Quality has two underpinnings:

☞ 1. Quality is a never-ending process. It's not a product; it's an outcome.

☞ 2. Quality is not determined by how good a product is at the start, but rather, what it's like at the finish.

Buying the most expensive piece of fish at the fish market does not mean it will be the highest-quality fish when it is served in the restaurant. Sure, it's important to buy the best quality you can afford, but it's the process that makes it an excellent entrée.

At the end of the meal, quality is defined by the stomach of the beholder!

We tell our people, "If you can't serve it with pride, you can't serve a quality dish, and if you can't serve a quality dish, you can't create a great customer memory."

Getting Started

"Do or do not. There is no try."

— YODA

CREATING URGENCY IS THE FIRST STEP IN MOBILIZING AN organization. According to Steve Robbins who writes the monthly column "The Leadership Workshop," fear mobilizes away from the danger.

He defines "away from" as "whichever direction someone is pointed when someone screams, 'Run!'" Everybody will move quickly — in whatever direction they are facing.

Fear gets people moving, but it won't get them moving in the same direction."

Fear does more harm than just scattering efforts; it also produces stress. Under stress, creativity vanishes, problem-solving abilities diminish, and people stop learning. They react based on impulse; they don't think through the consequences of their actions, and they become less able to spot patterns and interconnections.

That is fine for a five-minute burst of jungle adrenaline, but it won't create a workforce that can navigate a tricky economy. Working toward a larger purpose mobilizes people.

One of the most annoying whines I hear is about not having enough time to get everything done. If you watch those whiners work, you will find they give plenty of thought to what they want to do, but precious little thought to the sequence of events that will get them to their goal in the allocated time.

They say they don't have enough time, but they're wasting the time they have. Knowing how to get started is as important as knowing what you want to accomplish.

KNOW WHAT YOU'RE COOKING BEFORE YOU PICK YOUR POT

"In the long run, men hit only what they aim at."
— HENRY DAVID THOREAU

It is the unforced errors that typically cause a tennis player to lose a match. In business, it's false starts and lack of a goal that creates the most inefficiency.

Author Stephen Covey recommends that you make a habit of "beginning with the end in mind." But long before Covey published his first book, Sadie, a wonderful woman who cooked for my family when I was a child, told me, "Know what you're cooking before you pick your pot." (Besides dispensing wisdom, Sadie made the best mustard greens and sweet pickled pork you ever tasted.)

Plodders determine their ultimate destination. Then, before the journey begins, they develop a process to get there. They figure out what tools and support will be needed along the way.

CLEAN THE REFRIGERATOR

"Nothing ages like laziness."

— EDWARD BULWER-LYTTON

In the restaurant business, we regularly go through our refrigerators to make sure the products on the shelves aren't past their prime. At our restaurants, we do the same thing with every process. We regularly review how we are serving the customer to make sure we are creating great memories and meeting customer needs. We also continually look for ways to make our processes more cost-efficient so we can add greater value for our customers and create greater financial returns for our investors.

Just as important, we continually review the performance of all employees to make sure each person is still vital and remains an asset in creating great customer memories. We have learned the hard way that trying to hang onto staff members who have gone past their expiration date is like trying to keep milk months after it has spoiled.

Both outdated processes and employees past their expiration date create a sour smell. The sour smell of an outdated process is just a revolting as the odor of an employee gone bad. Either can make the whole kitchen stink if you don't do something about it fast.

At one time, Commander's Palace in New Orleans had a man considered one of the best maître d's in the world. George had been at Commander's more than 30 years. He started off shining shoes, then bussing tables, washing dishes, waiting tables, and finally, found his destiny at the front door.

He once received a $15,000 tip for taking care of a group after normal lunch hours.

The problem was that George was a superstar, not a team player. He resisted all organization and never found a rule he couldn't break. He was like the star of a Broadway show, waltzing in seconds before curtain time, then expecting to receive all the applause.

I told my mother for years that he was more trouble than he was worth, but she was reluctant to get rid of him. He was an institution. He had been in the refrigerator forever.

George left a couple of years ago after a customer set him up in business for himself. New Orleans reacted almost the same as when Archie Manning left the Saints. The story made front-page news.

When some of our best customers found out that George was no longer at Commander's Palace, they told us they were going to quit coming. But eventually they returned. Their relationship was with the restaurant, not just one person. Even without the superstar, the team we built earned those customers back.

Last Easter my mother confessed that I had been right. The front door at Commander's was the best it has ever been, and everyone associated with the front of the house was performing better than ever.

The news almost knocked me over. Delivering that "told you so" to my mother was one of the sweetest moments in my life.

Of course, people and processes aren't entirely like soured milk. They can become useful again. After the other restaurant failed, George returned to Commander's Palace — but this time, with the understanding that he'd be part of the team, not a soloist, and that we could get along just fine without him. Now he's a fresh employee all over again.

GET BUY-IN SOMEWHERE

"In the fight between you and the world, back the world."
— FRANK ZAPPA

Human nature resists change. So even when the change is to Plodding, you can't expect your entire organization to buy into it on Day One. Like a pot of red beans, Plodding takes time to develop.

You need momentum to get everyone on board. Obviously, momentum doesn't just happen. Think of your strategy as an avalanche which begins with one snowball rolling downhill.

As the leader, you have to take the first step by acting the way you want others to act. Then you need to get buy-in somewhere. Don't try to get it everywhere. Pick off the folks you can do something about.

First, get the right people together (you intuitively know who they are) and start making the right choices. Some right choices could include:

☞ Not expecting fast change, but girding for the long haul.

☞ Setting up a plan to seek to understand why your customers really do business with you despite the hurdles.

☞ Resisting the temptation to send people to training sessions, but rather, engaging your people in a learning process.

TALK ABOUT IT

"A fanatic is one who can't change his mind and won't change the subject."
— SIR WINSTON CHURCHILL

Once the course has been plotted, it's vital to consistently communicate it during the entire journey. Communication cures ambiguity, the greatest source of fear and mistrust.

Find ways for your philosophy to be included in every conversation you have with employees. This lets them know it's on the top of your mind and should be on the top of theirs. Point to it every time you see it happen so they will know what it looks like.

They may roll their eyes or even joke about it. But that's a sign of progress. I once told Chef Carl that I would know this was beginning to work when I heard people making jokes. People only do that about real things in their everyday lives.

Keep everyone posted on the progress being made. Spotlight the victories along the way. This builds momentum and reinforces the feeling that everyone is on the right track.

Periodically I send brief voicemail or e-mail messages to everyone on our staff who can receive them. The message may be a thank you, an online comment from one of our customers, an update, or even a note celebrating a Simple Truth victory. While the mass messages may be a little impersonal, at least people are able to hear my voice or read my words and know that we are still on track.

Leading a Plodding Organization

*"In a balanced organization, working towards
a common objective, there is success."*
— T.L. SCRUTTON

LEADING A PLODDING ORGANIZATION IS JUST LIKE LEADING any successful organization, except that it's different. The difference is not how you lead but how you believe. That may sound subtle, but it is the difference between success and failure.

A Plodding leader operates from the bottom of his or her soul, not from the top of the organizational pyramid. You have to believe it before you can understand it, and you have to live it before you can lead it.

IT BEGINS WITH FOLLOWSHIP

"A desk is a dangerous place from which to watch the world."
— JOHN LE CARRE

I have a problem with the concept of leadership that is in vogue today. My problem is not that I'm against people being leaders; it's just that leadership has become an end rather than a means. It's a position, rather than a process. It's a label, rather than a way of life.

In a staff meeting one day, I listened to the conversations around the table and heard all of the "right" leadership jargon being bandied about. It struck me that we were not meeting our business goals for lack of leadership; it was due to lack of followship.

Leadership is self-focused; followship is focused on others. As in customer service, the focus is on identifying people's needs. Understanding human nature will help you get employees where you want them to go — and to go there because it's also where *they* want to go.

Followship is also about giving up control and power. You can force people to shut their minds and march in step in one direction, but mindless marching is not the ultimate goal. The ultimate goal is having people walk with you on a journey because they want to, not because they have to.

Carl Walker, the executive chef at Brennan's of Houston, has great followship skills.

I first met Carl 20 years ago when he interviewed at Brennan's of Houston. I was impressed by him but did not have a position open, so I referred him to Mr. B's, one of my family's restaurants in New Orleans. He worked his way up through many kitchen assignments and eventually became executive sous chef at Commander's Palace.

In other words, he was second in command of the kitchen to a fellow named Emeril Lagasse. (Carl actually ran the kitchen while Emeril was out in the world, kicking it up a notch.)

In 1989 I had an opening for a chef in Houston. There was only one guy I wanted: Carl. Bringing him on board was one of the best decisions I ever made. Not just because he is a great chef, but also because he is a wonderful partner and engenders unconditional loyalty from his troops.

I have learned a lot from Carl and with Carl. All through my Simple Truth journey, Carl was my alter ego, the wall to bounce ideas off, the confidant with whom I could share my hopes and reveal my fears.

He was sometimes skeptical, fearing that I was unleashing yet another miracle cure. When he believed an idea was good, he would tell me. His honesty helped me forge the honest philosophy that continues to work and improve with age.

I learned about leadership, and consequently followship, from Carl because I could observe a role model in action, not in some simulated classroom situation, but in the heat of battle.

Teaching is why people work for Carl for less money. They know they are getting more out of the bargain than a paycheck. If people will take less money to learn, then it follows that giving of one's self is a very powerful tool.

Carl teaches by giving. He doesn't hand people a cookbook or manual and then send them off on their own. He role-models, and he lives what he teaches. Carl epitomizes the truism: "People don't care how much you know until they know how much you care."

He keeps in touch with a corps of former employees who have moved on and, mostly, up. They continue to come to him for advice and counsel. And no matter how busy he is, Carl finds time for those who seek him out, whether they work for him today or left his kitchen years ago.

If you don't have followship, you're not leading the parade. You are the parade.

DON'T TAKE RESPONSIBILITY, GIVE IT.

Never tell people how to do things. Tell them what to do and they will surprise you with their ingenuity."

— GEORGE PATTON

I believe people follow when they need to go to a different place, and they are willing to take responsibility for their choices in getting there. Successful leaders help people make choices and accept responsibility for the consequences of their choices.

Confident employees take charge of their jobs. Michael Jordan wanted the ball when the game was on the line — not because he was panicked that no one else could make the basket, but because he had passion and confidence that he could get the job done. (My mother calls it a sense of urgency, and she does not gladly suffer anyone one who lacks it.)

Young leaders often feel compelled to take responsibility for the performance of their people. Maybe they've seen too many war movies where the gung-ho squadron leader stands before the general and proclaims that as the leader, he alone is responsible for the failed mission.

But by taking the blame, the leader is also taking responsibility away from the people he supervises. He renders them drones and perpetuates the victim excuse.

Giving responsibility to workers down the line also helps to ward off management burnout. Managers don't have to solve all the problems and make all the decisions. Everyone takes responsibility for the problem and getting the customer to return.

Most of us have been raised in the old management model where the benevolent boss proclaimed he had an open-door policy and encouraged people to bring their problems so he could help solve them. That doesn't work in a Plodding organization.

Begin by telling every employee that you don't want to hear their problems; you only want to hear their solutions to their problems. Your door is open, but only to help them work through solutions and alternatives and coach them how to make the right choice.

TRUTH AND TECHNOLOGY

"He that will not apply new remedies must expect new evils."
— FRANCIS BACON

At our restaurants, we embrace technology — but only if the technology helps achieve us achieve our Simple Truth.

Our reservation system, for instance, is high-tech, but also high-touch. The title of a hit by country-music star Kenny Chesney could be about creating great customer memories: "You Had Me From Hello." If we don't hook our customers from the "hello" of their first phone call, our task is difficult when they reach the restaurant.

Part of our strategy is purely human. Usually when you call to reserve a table at a restaurant, the first question you're asked is, When would you like to join us? At Brennan's of Houston, we begin instead by asking the customer's name. From the customer's perspective, we are taking things in the right order — his. We will get the details we need, but the customer knows he comes first.

At that point, our technology, ReservationSource by Guest-Bridge Software, comes into play. Until just a few years ago, like everyone else in the restaurant industry, we wrote reservations in a book. Now our reservationist types the first few letters of the customer's last name on a computer terminal.

Instantly the system searches the database, and if the customer is listed there, the reservationist clicks on the name, and opens a file with data we've gathered from previous visits — likes, dislikes, favorite wines and dishes. She then takes the date, time and number in the party. The system reviews the table matrix and gives her the best option for taking that reservation.

After taking the reservation on the phone, we can e-mail a confirmation if the customer likes. This eliminates the time-consuming (and often annoying) need for us to call the customer the day before to reconfirm.

"No-shows," as they are known in the business, are extremely costly. If the customer does not show up, the table sits empty. We not only lose revenue, but it appears to our other guests that our business is hurting. Anything we can do to communicate with our customer and, more important, allow him to communicate with us, reduces that unrecoverable cost.

The day's reservations are shown on the computer screen, and they can be printed for those who don't like looking at computer screens. Either option eliminates the embarrassed "I'm sure I saw your name here somewhere" speeches from the reservationist as she tries to decipher multiple handwriting styles in different colors of ink and pencil smudges.

Our dining rooms are also mapped on the computer screen, allowing us to accurately track where every customer is as well as table turn times. This is our version of the control tower at an airport.

But the system does not stop there. In baseball, great hitters keep a "book" on every pitcher so that they know his tendencies. We do the same for our special customers.

The information helps the entire service team to do a better job. Before the customer arrives, a copy of his profile is given to those closest to the customer's experience, the servers and cooks.

If a customer is new to us, we create a file for him and gather information during service. We note where he sat, who served him, what he ate and drank, as well as particulars such as food allergies.

The servers add information to the sheets they are given and complete the information loop by returning the annotated sheets to management. We track which employees are participating in our in-house marketing and reward them.

Through technology, we have found a way to tell both our customers and our employees that we value them as people. This has created a new paradigm for our business. (No business book is complete without one use of the word "paradigm!") The technology makes us more hospitable, and hospitality connects us to the customer. Each works better together than separately.

RELEASE THE WATER UNDER THE BRIDGE

"The weak can never forgive. Forgiveness is the attribute of the strong."
— MAHATMA GANDHI

Human nature causes us all to want to move past awkward moments quickly, and if possible, totally avoid confrontation. The expression "It's just water under the bridge" is a diplomatic way to say, "You've wronged me, but I'd rather not talk about it, and I just want it to go away."

The problem is, past wrongs don't just go away. Water under the bridge doesn't disappear. It eventually flows somewhere else.

Being from New Orleans, I understand the importance of levees. They are constructed to hold back the waters that have gone under the bridge and end up in the reservoir. Levees don't break when the sun is shining. They break during severe storms.

It's the same in business. All the drops of awkwardness and confrontational issues end up in a reservoir, putting pressure on the levee. Eventually, those raindrops add up to a flood, and they can knock down the levee.

Inevitably, a flood comes when we are least prepared to deal with it. And that is typically when the customer is there to see it happen.

The fabulous motivational speaker Amanda Gore notes that you need to establish a relationship with someone in order to feel comfortable airing your complaints. In one presentation, she talks about "building a bridge and getting over it."

If you don't build the bridge, you obviously can't get over it, and you can't get over it until you finish building it. It doesn't happen fast, and it is hard work. Once the bridge is built, each person must choose to get over it, let the grievances go, and forgive.

Some years ago, early in our relationship, Carl Walker and I had reached a breaking point. We had let the little stresses of business accumulate until finally, fed up with one another, we began one of those conversations that could easily have ended with his quitting. He'd have lost a job. I'd have lost my executive chef and a friend.

We had the good sense to take the discussion out of our workplace. At Griff's, a neighborhood watering hole, we drank scotch and vented our resentments. Luckily, we had enough of a relationship (and enough scotch) not to let the conversation go too far.

Since then, we've occasionally let minor resentments build up, but never for long. We know better now.

NEVER ASK MY OPINION

"Opinions that are well rooted should grow and change like a healthy tree."
— IRVING BATCHELLER

The Simple Truth has become my silent partner, and I have found that the more I am silent, the stronger the partnership is.

By living the Simple Truth, I eliminate the need for employees to ask my opinion. They know that every decision at Brennan's of Houston comes back to one guiding question: Does it make great customer memories?

Not having to answer questions all day long not only is a stress reliever for me, it assures that decisions are made quickly and on the spot.

TEACH, DON'T TRAIN

"Originality is nothing but judicious imitation."
— VOLTAIRE

There is a big difference between training and teaching. Training involves someone having the answer and attempting to impart that knowledge to others. Training is something done to people. On the other hand, teaching is something you do *with* people.

There are no hired trainers at our restaurants; there's only "us." The people in the line of fire teach the people who are in the line of fire. The generals on the hill have to come down from the hill on a regular basis.

The teacher always gets more out of the process than the student. Helping people learn makes you to think about what you are saying before you say it. Teaching forces you to re-examine your beliefs and to re-live your experiences. Teaching keeps your learning fresh and at the front of your mind, not buried in the recesses.

Our learning sessions are really more like discussion groups. We all get in a room and talk about a pre-determined topic. Everyone knows the topic in advance so they can prepare their questions and ideas.

But learning sessions are considered a secondary process. The primary learning technique takes place one-on-one, and in the line of duty, not in some isolated room.

Our type of learning is "feeling it" rather than "hearing it."

I make it a point to teach the new-hire orientation session. I have learned that my taking the time with new people is one of the best uses of my time. It is clear from the beginning that I am serious about the Simple Truth way of life. My managers also tell me that it is a great way to show support for them.

Learning is not an event. It is a way of life.

DRIVE-BY MENTORING

"There cannot be greater rudeness than to interrupt another in the current of his discourse."
— JOHN LOCKE

I believe in being out among the troops when they are experiencing the moments of truth. To me, that's the best time to mentor.

But I've learned to be careful about my timing. Ideas excite me, and I love to share them. I used to hijack my people in moments when I was very enthusiastic about a particular breakthrough. I wanted to get it out on the table and get going with it.

While my intentions were good, most of the time I wasn't getting good vibes or body language from my abductees. Finally, during a hijacking of one of my long-term employees, I asked what was wrong.

His response still resonates with me today: "Alex, I like talking to you about ideas and all, but it's like you catch me in a 'drive-by.' You come at me out of the blue with all this energy, and I'm never ready or prepared for it. In fact, you are usually interrupting me when it happens."

I was not taking into account the person's frame of mind or schedule. I was being arrogant, thinking that what he was doing could not possibly be as important as what I had on my mind. Once I began scheduling these discussions and giving folks a preview before the meeting, I not only got the good vibes I was hoping for, I got the enthusiasm I wanted.

GUIDE TO A SUCCESSFUL
MEETING WITH ALEX

"Be sincere; be brief; be seated."
— FRANKLIN D. ROOSEVELT

On the wall behind my desk hangs a sign: "Guide to a Successful Meeting with Alex." It succinctly summarizes the questions any Plodder should ask of any proposal.

☞ 1. How does it affect the Simple Truth of our business (creating Great Memories for our Guests)?

☞ 2. Does it fit with our P's & Q?

☞ 3. Have you discussed your idea with others?

☞ 4. Do you have a plan to follow through and determine if this idea works or creates value?

☞ 5. If you have answered "yes" to questions 1-4, why are you asking me?

ONE TRUTH, ONE SCORECARD

Two men working as a team will produce
more than three men working as individuals."
— CHARLES P. MCCORMICK

A key to our success has been changing the employee performance scorecard to be totally in sync with our Simple Truth.

Like many successful businesses, we have a performance-review system. We want our employees always to know how they are performing. By clearly articulating management's expectations, we hold them accountable for their own decisions and the results those decisions deliver.

Before discovering our Simple Truth, we had scorecards for each department. The wait staff had different criteria from did the kitchen staff, whose criteria were different from the banquet staff. They were rewarded for different, and sometimes conflicting, measurements. Everybody had a different goal line.

After adopting our Simple Truth, we quickly concluded that we needed one scorecard for everyone. So we spent countless hours developing elaborate charts and systems to be used to coach each employee category.

After spending much valuable time trying to find a scorecard that measured every variable, we realized that there was only one perfect scorecard, and it was the only one that mattered to our customers — making a great memory.

We now have one scorecard for every person at our restaurants — even me.

Our scorecard is totally focused on what makes us successful. How did you do at creating great customer memories?

Sure, we do budgets by department, and we track costs, revenue, and overhead just like any other successful business. We hold people accountable for their commitments and for the budgets they develop for their areas. But no matter the budget, no matter the plan, no matter the short-term impact on revenue, every person makes immediate decisions based on a single criterion: What can I do to make sure each customer leaves with great memories?

Creating great customer memories is everyone's ultimate job, whether she works directly with customers or supports the people who do.

Obviously, not everyone can be measured directly on creating customer memories in every aspect of their job. For instance, we evaluate cooks by checking how many dishes come back and their ability to control food costs. To level the playing field, we reward longer-term employees with higher pay and better schedules and give them a say in how their area runs. We do, however, hold cooks accountable for how they treat their customers — the servers. They must treat them as well as the wait staff treats guests in the dining room.

Going to this single scorecard approach, we have seen three huge benefits:

☞ 1. Everyone is working toward the same goal line.
☞ 2. Everyone understands that the only acceptable behavior is working together and being totally cooperative. There are no departments or job descriptions when it

comes to creating a great customer memory. Either we did or we didn't.

☞ 3. Everyone clearly understands how he or she adds value to the business and why he or she is just as important as the next person on the team.

Having one scorecard also allows each person to manage himself rather than be managed by the boss. When there is totally clarity and absolute simplicity, there is no place for anyone to hide.

Why Hospitality Matters

Getting Connected

"It is so simple a remedy, merely service. The call is for nobility of thinking, nobility of doing. The call is for service, and such is the wholesomeness of it. He who serves all, best serves himself."
— JACK LONDON

IN THIS E-COMMERCE, ATM-DRIVEN WORLD, PEOPLE ARE starved for convivial human contact. And because such moments are rare, each one becomes all the more important. Customers care deeply how you treat them.

No matter if you are selling cars, office supplies or financial services, your business will succeed only if you are outstanding at pleasing customers. No customer ever said, "I can't wait to do more business with them. They treat me as if I don't matter."

The business battle cry is to "get connected," but if misused, new technologies can leave the customer less connected to a business. Your primary connection should not be to the Internet or the network, but rather, to the customer. The connection is not a wire, Wi-Fi, or an infrared beam. It's hospitality.

That's why you need to understand hospitality.

Hospitality matters because the customer says it does.

Hospitality is one of those terms that everyone thinks he understands. But all too often, when people hear the word "hospitality," they limit the definition to serving food and drinks to people in restaurants, bars, and hotels — in other words, the "hospitality industry." Many businesspeople don't understand the essence of the term, or how it applies to their business.

Hospitality is like customer service with a double dose of caffeine.

It's the same as customer service in that the task is to satisfy customers' desires and meet their needs. But hospitality feels different from customer service because it is delivered with passion and truth. It is not perfunctory, but rather, innate service.

Mix in all of the clichés: The customer is the boss/king/only reason we exist; service is not what you do, it's how you do it, etc. Then add the caffeine-like ingredients of "now," "passion" and "attitude," and the recipe comes to life.

The difference between customer service and hospitality is that hospitality is the attitude with which you embrace the customer as a friend in your own "home," whether that home is your restaurant, bar, hotel, front office, sales floor, airplane or telephone.

Hospitality happens in the urgency of the now. It happens between people, not between businesses.

Hospitality is the human connection that holds the service chain together. It is the eyeball-to-eyeball, immediate response that puts a face on service.

Fortunately, hospitality can be learned, but it cannot be faked.

HOSPITALITY IN A GLASS

"The only proper intoxication is conversation."
— OSCAR WILDE

One evening my wife and I hosted a friend and his wife for dinner at our restaurant. My friend's wife asked for a glass of blonde Lillet, an apéritif that is seldom ordered. When she found we did not have it, she ordered a glass of wine. She appeared pleased, and the evening went on. About 15 minutes later, in walked my service captain, who quietly placed a glass of blonde Lillet in front of her.

Of course she was astonished. Without anyone asking him to do so, he had driven in his own car to the liquor store down the street and even used his own money to buy the apéritif. (Of course he knew I would reimburse him!)

Did he do it because I was at the table? No, the smile on his face told me he got much more out of it himself than any "atta boy" I could have given him. He wanted to make her feel like a special guest which she certainly did.

About two weeks later, that customer booked a party for twenty people, proving that it pays to be hospitable!

HOSPITALITY IN A STORM

*"Bounty always receives part of its value
from the manner in which it is bestowed."*
— SAMUEL JOHNSON

In 2001, Tropical Storm Allison struck Houston with little warning. The city was flooded, and about a dozen of our customers were stranded all night at Brennan's of Houston. Our employees chose to make the best of a bad situation and did their best to make our guests at home. The employees kept the food and the coffee coming and poured from the bar with our compliments. (None of the guests took advantage.) The employees fashioned bedding out of tablecloths. They monitored the water level in the streets and helped people decide whether it was safe to leave.

Our employees could have gone through the motions. They could have spent the night talking only to each other and watching the TV. Instead, they went the extra mile. They weren't told to do so. But they felt great the next day.

The McDonald's Syndrome

"It requires a certain kind of mind to see beauty in a hamburger bun."
— RAY KROC

IT IS FOOLISH TO BELIEVE THAT PEOPLE WHO HAVE NOT experienced hospitality can deliver it. The majority of today's front-line workers have been raised experiencing and expecting McDonald's vision of service and hospitality. You stand in a line until you reach the counter where you encounter a teenage counter clerk who only wants to know which pre-packaged, pre-cooked menu option you want. No substitutions!

McDonald's is an interesting microcosm of today's hospitality and customer service puzzle. McDonald's has routinized service and food preparation to the point that it encourages the service people not to think, just perform, and perform inside very stringent parameters.

McDonald's extols the team concept, but a McDonald's server seems to focus solely on his assigned task. He may realize he is a link in a chain, but he cares only about how his individual task links with the ones before and after his.

The counter staff is trained to smile, but to smile while staying within the system. The customer is expected to know before reaching the counter what she wants to order, but if she isn't sure, the staff member points to a large, confusing menu board. McDonald's culture emphasizes conformity and operational convenience rather than customer convenience. And it definitely does not meet my definition of hospitality!

Recently, *Fortune* described how Jim Cantalupo, the new CEO of McDonald's, was planning to turn around the company that once was one of the most respected American icons in the world. McDonald's had announced its first-ever quarterly loss in January, 2003, and same-store sales had been falling for nearly a year. Perhaps it should have come as no surprise: On the University of Michigan's Customer-Satisfaction Index, McDonald's had ranked at the bottom for nearly a decade.

In the article, Cantalupo said he planned to get back to basics and focus on the customer. Obviously, I applaud that strategy.

But I worried that he hadn't thought it through. He admitted that many McDonald's stores have fallen into disrepair, but he said the company would not sink too much of its capital into store renovation because now more than 60 percent of all McDonald's transactions take place at the drive-through window.

In other words, Cantalupo is willing to sacrifice the experience of the nearly half of McDonald's customers who still eat inside the stores.

And really, how good is the experience at the drive-through? The store's culture extends there, too. The customer stops first at a talking speaker box, then twice more at windows where unmotivated workers shove orders out the window. At best, the experience is painless. But it doesn't build a relationship.

McDonald's has announced that it may drop the slogan "We love to see you smile" because it hasn't increased sales. But I don't think the ads are to blame nearly as much as the company's culture and its lack of hospitality. The ad doesn't work because it doesn't ring true. McDonald's people feel — and act — as if they are cogs in a huge, impersonal machine. And naturally, that feeling shows in the way they treat the customer.

McDonald's is hardly alone. Like McDonald's, many huge, monolithic corporations pretend to deliver individualized customer service by creating uniform service protocols and procedures that are reduced to writing and distributed to each store in a policy manual. (The so-called "innovative" companies now put the policy manual on the Internet so they can tell their shareholders they are into "distance learning.") The absentee owners frown on spontaneity and fun. The lowest common denominator becomes the highest priority.

Sadly, customers have learned to expect less. But when did this snowball of awful service start downhill? There was once a great American tradition of service going back to the mom-and-pop establishments where business owners lived above their stores. They stayed close to what mattered most — the customer, and the customer experience.

Once people experience true hospitality, they intuitively "get it." But the McDonald's generation may never have experienced it. So how can we ask employees to deliver hospitality if they have never experienced it?

At my restaurants, we have found that the best way to teach hospitality is to role-model it and then reward it. When people around you are acting hospitable to the customer and to each other, it's a lot easier to understand and much easier to do.

Puttin' on the Ritz

"Inns are the mirror and at the same time the flower of the people."
— HILLAIRE BELLOC

A SIMILAR ATTITUDE PREVAILS AT THE RITZ-CARLTON HOTELS and restaurants. The Ritz-Carlton not only delivers one of the finest service experiences in the hospitality industry, it is the only hotel company to win the prestigious Malcolm Baldridge Award of Excellence. And just to prove how outstanding they are, the Ritz-Carlton has won the Baldridge Award twice!

The Ritz-Carlton vision statement is: "Ladies and gentlemen serving ladies and gentlemen." I believe the Ritz-Carlton's success is due not only to having a great vision statement, but also to the disciplined, thorough manner in which they live the statement, and subsequently, how they hire and train their people.

The Ritz-Carlton buys the same beds as does the Hilton or Marriott. They buy their food ingredients from the same supplier as most restaurants in town. They even serve the same liquor and wine as the other top restaurants and bars in the market.

So how do they get such premium prices for a night at their hotel? Very simply, it is the Ritz-Carlton brand of hospitality that separates them from everyone else and attracts guests who will gladly pay $400 a night for a single room.

The Ritz-Carlton does not pay its service staff much more than other hotels do. So how does a person who makes $25,000 a year understand how to deliver the level of service expected by someone who pays $400 a night for a room and $6 a glass for the same iced tea that the Holiday Inn serves?

The answer lies in how they live their vision statement. They treat their people like ladies and gentlemen so their people know what it means.

The Ritz-Carlton understands the impact of human nature on the bottom line. Treat people as if they're special, and they will act special — and treat others like they are special. They also walk the talk of empowering their employees to meet the needs of customers on the spot. There are three tenets to Ritz-Carlton empowerment:

☞ Move heaven and earth to satisfy a customer.

☞ Each employee has spending authority of $2000 to solve a customer problem.

☞ Every employee has the authority to call in a co-worker for help.

According to their web site, "By applying the principles of trust, honest, respect, integrity and commitment we nurture and maximize talent to the benefit of each individual and the company. The Ritz-Carlton fosters a work environment where diversity is valued, quality of life is enhanced, individual aspirations are fulfilled, and The Ritz-Carlton mystique is strengthened."

And the Ritz-Carlton leadership understands the need for recruiting the right kind of people and putting them through the right kind of training. They go out of their way to find people who want to be the best, are uncompromising, love people and are team players. They want to be part of the family instead of a link in a rigid McDonald's-like process.

Those new hires receive intense training — at least 250 hours in their first year — and are paired with a seasoned employee. They learn "The Ritz-Carlton Basics," 20 brief lines explaining what running a hotel is all about. Every day every member of the staff has a daily quality line-up meeting with his boss. And every day the company picks one of the 20 basics for everyone on the staff to discuss.

The Ritz-Carlton has succinctly defined its core customer and its target employee. The hotel serves people who want and expect to be treated like ladies and gentlemen and who will gladly pay to receive that treatment.

The Ritz-Carlton has not mastered the hotel business; they have mastered the hospitality business. And whether you have an accounting firm, manufacturing plant or run a government agency, your business will improve when you decide you are in the hospitality business as well.

Harness
Human Nature

The Power
of Human Nature

"The employer generally gets the employees he deserves"
— SIR WALTER BILBEY

NO MATTER HOW HARD I TRIED AS A MANAGER, I COULD NOT change people. I learned the hard way that people have to change themselves.

Management pressure for an employee to change creates resistance, and resistance causes most business-improvement failures. It's as if an oppositional reflex has been ingrained in the DNA through years of unenlightened managers battling employees.

People almost always act in what they perceive to be their own self-interest, and unless you can prove that your course of action is best for your employees as individuals, they won't do what you want. That's human nature. And that's never going to change.

Human nature is the most powerful force on earth. You can use it to move your business forward or to stop it dead in its tracks. The secret of successful management is to embrace human nature — your employees' human nature, your customers', and your own — and understand how it fits with your business. You can harness human nature, or it will harness you.

WHAT PEOPLE WANT

"Most of us have a pretty clear idea of the world we want.
What we lack is an understanding of how to go about getting it."
— HUGH GIBSON

Here's what I have found that people want most at work:

☞ They want to know what is expected of them and how
they will be rewarded for meeting those expectations.

☞ They want management to do what management says
and stop saying what management is going to do.

☞ They want to know the role they play in the company's success and that their contribution is vital and appreciated.

☞ They want to be given the opportunity to get ahead,
and they want to know how they are progressing on a
regular basis.

☞ They want to be told the truth and have access to relevant
information that affects their job and/or their lives.

☞ Perhaps most of all, they want to know that management
cares.

At our restaurants, we call this list the Employees' Bill of
Rights.

WHAT'S IN IT FOR ME?

"Nothing great was ever achieved without enthusiasm."

— RALPH WALDO EMERSON

When a manager proposes change, an employee automatically thinks, "What's in it for me?" That's not a selfish question, nor is it egocentric. It's just human nature.

To pass the "What's In It For Me" test, you must be able to answer the question from the perspective of each individual in the organization. The sales manager's payoff is not the same as the forklift driver's, or the pharmacy manager's. The hotdog vendor and the All-Star pitcher have dramatically different points of view.

You must overcome employees' automatic suspicion of anything that comes from the top, an old problem grown worse in this post-Enron era. They suspect corporate skulduggery and feel sure that the boys in the back office are out to get the little guys. You must convince them that the Simple Truth is in not only in management's best interests but in theirs.

You must show, too, that the customer's interest runs parallel to the employee's — that giving terrific customer service will be rewarded. To use my "railroading" analogy, those two tracks must remain perfectly parallel; if they diverge even a tiny bit, people can get hurt.

Of course, different groups' interests are not exactly the same. An initiative that generates substantial profit for the business may put no extra money in employees' pockets.

So how do you convince employees to embrace a project that might mean significant increases in compensation for the owner and the senior management, but not for people further down the line?

Let me give an example. At our restaurants, we sell cookbooks to many of our customers. They provide a nice profit margin for the owners, but the staff does not get a tip or extra compensation.

For the staff, the "What's In It For Me" benefit is pride in working at a restaurant so good that people want to take home a piece of it. For other initiatives, the "What's In It For Me" benefit might be better working conditions or an easier service process, or pride in working for the most successful restaurant in town.

The benefits are often more emotional that rational. Money is a rational benefit, but seldom is it a person's main motivation to change.

The Need
for Connection

*"Never continue in a job you don't enjoy. If you're happy in what
you're doing, you'll like yourself, you'll have inner peace.
And if you have that, along with physical health, you will have had
more success than you could possibly have imagined."*
— JOHNNY CARSON

A FEW YEARS AGO I HAD THE OPPORTUNITY TO HEAR A FORMER
Vietnam prisoner of war speak about his experience. His speech
haunted me for days.

The North Vietnamese kept the POWs in small cells made of
concrete blocks. They barely had enough room to stretch out to
sleep. They were forbidden to talk to each other, but not even
their captors could stop the power of human nature and the
need to be connected.

The prisoners developed a communication system similar
to Morse code. They used any hard item they could find to bang
on the walls of their cells. Every day at sunset, each would bang
out a message to the man in the next cell, in part, just to let him
know that his cellmate was still alive, that he wasn't alone.

To a man, every POW who returned home said that feeling of
being connected was what kept him alive. And to this day, every
POW from that prison can still beat out that rudimentary code!

Communication kept the POWs alive. And it's how people stay connected at work as well.

Poor managers spend a lot of time saying, "Just focus on your job and don't worry about the other guy." But in fact, you *want* your employees to worry about the other guy and to worry about him in the right way.

At our restaurants, we didn't see a real increase in productivity until we turned the focus from the individual to the team and turned the team's focus to what the customer really wants.

THE 359-DEGREE CIRCLE

"Coming together is a beginning; keeping together is progress; working together is success."

— HENRY FORD

And how do you get people to work as a team? Our approach is the "359-degree circle." We explain that a true circle is 360 degrees and ask people to visualize the rest of the team as the 359 degrees. Each person is the one degree that completes the circle. If each person doesn't perform his or her role, the circle does not close.

When hiring people to join our circle, we focus on two characteristics: talent and attitude. Talent, of course, is the innate ability to excel at the position.

Attitude matters even more than talent. If the attitude is there, we have managers who are outstanding coaches and can help people develop the skills to deliver "great memories" service. But attitude itself cannot be trained; it must first exist for us to be able to bring it out. Another word for "attitude" is "passion." We want people who are passionate about our serving customers. We want people who are looking for something beyond a paycheck.

We keep in mind that both talent and attitude are hard to gauge through past job performance. Early in my career I made the mistake of focusing only on skills and related experience. It was what everyone else did, and I felt safe following the crowd.

Once I gained the confidence to hire applicants with no previous restaurant experience, I began to find some of our best people. In my restaurants, it's not uncommon to find sous chefs with doctoral degrees in comparative literature or physics. You might find former actors, engineers, law students, and construction workers. A star service person may have had four diverse careers before finding his place in the food-service business.

One of our most valuable players is Santino Pirelli. He runs the front door at Commander's Palace in Las Vegas. Virtually every customer raves about the great Santino.

Prior to joining our team, Santino was in the hair business. His mother had been a hairdresser in Italy, and along with her and his brothers, he owned a salon in Chicago. Once he figured out the hair business was not for him, he bounced around looking for a job that excited him, and for a company that made him feel appreciated. He was searching for a job that allowed his passion to come out.

Once we explained the Secret Truth to him and told him he would be accountable for his personal performance, he lit up brighter than all the lights on the Strip.

He says that we give him free reign to do things his way, as long as his way fits creates a great customer memory. Working the door of Commander's Palace Las Vegas, Santino knows how to let people love him and to feel loved by him. After he gets to know you, he always greets you with a heartfelt hug. Hundreds of customers have told me that Santino made their day. In other words, he made a memory.

STEPHAN A. VELAZQUEZ
ESTHER M. VELAZQUEZ

June 26, 2003

Santino Perrelli
Maitre D'
Commander's Palace
3663 Las Vegas Blvd. South, Suite 730
Las Vegas, NV 89109

Dear Santino,

Esther and I had dinner on June 5, (our 21ˢᵗ anniversary) at your restaurant. It was a very special night for us and it began with your exceptionally warm greeting. Your greeting was so warm and genuine, I wondered if you recognized Esther or me and we were old friends. The entire evening was outstanding and the finish on your restaurant truly brings elegance from New Orleans to Las Vegas.

Thank you again and we hope to see you soon.

Warmest regards,

Stephan Velazquez
Esther Velazquez

We let him do things his way — a very non-standard way — at the front door of a multi-million-dollar business. Because we earned Santino's trust and respect, he became passionate about his role. He feels appreciated and knows that what he is doing makes a difference. He didn't feel that way cutting hair.

But what about people who've already performed jobs similar to the ones they're applying for — and performed those jobs badly? We still consider them. Many of our star employees had been labeled poor performers and bad-attitude dudes at other restaurants. First, we found that most had been burned by poor organizational systems in which they couldn't, or wouldn't, buy into the program. They aren't bad people; they were just at the wrong place.

All they need is a way to focus on what makes them unique, combined with an atmosphere that celebrates and rewards their uniqueness. They need to be aligned with human nature, not put in positions that oppose it.

When they come to understand that the Simple Truth allows them to be who they are without having to fight the system, they respond with passion, commitment and honesty. When people follow their passion, they are happy. They show up at work because they want to, rather than because they have to. They leave when the job is done, and not when the whistle blows. And just as important, they attract other passionate people.

Once we have decided to offer a job, but before we seal the deal, we spend a good deal of time talking with the potential hire about our Simple Truth and how we expect he will live it. That way, there are no surprises once he is on board, and we have a jump-start in our teaching and learning process.

DON'T HIRE SUPERSTARS OR INDIVIDUALS

"The important thing to recognize is that it takes a team,
and the team ought to get credit for the wins and losses.
Successes have many fathers, failures have none."
— PHILIP CALDWELL

The 359-degree approach explains who we hire — and also who we don't hire. We do not want superstars at our restaurants. Nor do we want individuals. We succeed or fail as a team, so we're looking for team players. We want to be Jim Haslett's Saints, not Mike Ditka's.

Sure, I want people who want to be All-Stars, and I will give them the support to be all they can be. I just don't want them becoming All-Stars at the expense of others on the team or at the expense of the well-oiled machine we have created. The key lies in getting superstars to focus on succeeding with others, not in spite of them.

When you reward performance above all else, you get performance at the expense of all else. And you attract people who want to win at any price, ethical or not. At best, superstars can destroy your corporate culture and any efforts to inspire team feeling. At worst, they can bring down your company.

Enron's culture eventually became based on individual performance. Outlandish compensation schemes overly rewarded the person making the deal rather than the people delivering the product to the customer. Success at the expense of all else was not only tolerated, it was rewarded. People were urged to be superstars.

A handful of those superstars eventually brought the company down. And sadly, all of the hard-working 359-degree people went down with them, losing their jobs, and pensions.

One of my own superstars was a bartender that I'll call Sam. He was the best bartender that I'd ever seen. He held court while some of the city's wealthiest and most powerful individuals sat entranced. He could make any drink a customer could think of.

But he acted as if the rules didn't apply to him. He came in late. He left his paperwork incomplete at best and broke almost every rule in the book.

I let Sam stay for 15 years because I valued what he brought, and I thought it was worthwhile to clean up behind him. I was wrong.

SINK RUSTY SHIPS

"And the trouble is, if you don't risk anything, you risk even more."
— ERICA JONG "

Sometimes a problem staff member needs a nudge toward the door.

A recent TV news story gave me a chuckle. The Navy was preparing to sink a decommissioned ship off the coast of Florida to create an artificial reef and sport-diving attraction. Much was being made about this plan, as it was to be the largest ship intentionally sunk to create a reef. The Navy and the community furiously debated the plan's environmental impact, and the plan proceeded at a typical bureaucratic pace.

Finally the demolition experts boarded the ship to put the explosives in place. Before they could finish, the ship sank on its own in the ship channel, and the explosives team had to be rescued by a nearby tugboat much to the delight of the hovering news crews.

It seems that the bottom of the ship had finally rusted to the point that the ship could no longer float, and it sank in the worst possible place.

The moral of the story is that if you sit around and talk long enough, rust will sink your ship as surely as a torpedo. Bad employees are like rust on a ship. If you don't remove them quickly, they will sink your business.

Sam, the superstar bartender, was a rusty ship. Finally, my management team decided to fire him.

When the staff heard, everyone was concerned that his absence might hurt our bar business. But mainly, the staff was relieved. Only then did I realize how much Sam had held others back.

Immediately after the sinking, our bar business dropped off. We lost some regulars, but to our delight, they didn't stay gone long. After a brief dip, the bar volume returned and even showed a slight increase.

We were on the right course, and the decision was confirmed when readers of the restaurant publication *My Table* voted Brennan's of Houston as having the "Best Bar Service" in the city.

I shudder to think how much money and productivity we lost by letting so much rust form on our ship.

SOME JUST HAVE TO EXPERIENCE IT

"There are some people that, if they don't know, you can't tell them."
— LOUIS ARMSTRONG

Some people are too skeptical to buy into any new initiative. One of my managers — we'll call him Ray — was a "if you want something done right" kind of guy. Ray's attitude toward his staff was "This is as good as it gets, and it's not going to get any better."

But Ray was a great purchasing manager and got more done by 9:00 a.m. than most people do in a day. In addition to buying everything we needed to deliver great memories, he managed the ware-washing staff, not exactly the most service-oriented department.

Ray didn't think he had a dog in the "Great Customer Memories" fight. He was willing to go along with the internal part because he wanted to make the job better for his guys, but that was as far as it went.

He was skeptical about the whole improvement process. He just didn't see how it made money. He participated in the process, but he expressed his skepticism in water-cooler chat. He never went against the effort, but he never got out in front of it, either. It became obvious to everyone that a leader was not on board.

Then an extraordinary service experience put Ray's resistance in the spotlight. He was scheduled to attend a black-tie industry event and had gone to our formal-wear supplier to get everything he needed for that night. At least, he thought he was getting everything he needed.

As he was getting dressed for the function, he realized there was no tux shirt in the garment bag. He called our supplier, but found they had been closed for hours. He rushed to the Yellow Pages and found a listing for Men's Wearhouse.

He called the store nearest him. The salesman answering the phone told Ray that the store had been closed for an hour, but the salesman said he'd help Ray if he hurried over. The salesman not only sold Ray the shirt he needed; he pressed it before Ray left.

Later, Ray wrote a letter to Men's Wearhouse president George Zimmer. He didn't expect a response, but Mr. Zimmer wrote back to thank him for his positive comments.

Ray confided to me that he had thought the ads touting Men's Wearhouse service were just advertising hot air. But after his great service experience, he told many of us about it in an "I'll be damned" tone of voice. He paid more attention to what we were doing and tried to get on board and be a leader.

SOMETIMES EXPERIENCING IT ISN'T ENOUGH

"Every problem has a gift for you in its hands."
— RICHARD BACH

Though Ray improved dramatically after his Men's Wearhouse experience, he just couldn't live the Simple Truth. It was against his nature.

No good employee leaves for any one reason. Ray had a lot going on in his life and a desire to grow. But as the Simple Truth began to catch on, he became less comfortable.

He came to me one day and said, "I get it, and I understand it, but it's just not for me. I'm going to leave."

I was disappointed. But I was pleased that he felt comfortable enough to have that conversation with me, rather than just disappearing into the night which is often how restaurant employees leave a job.

I was also pleased to see the culture working. If you can't live it, our culture forces you out. That's what harnessing human nature does.

Plan for the Worst

"Behold the turtle. He makes progress only when he sticks his neck out."
— JAMES B. CONANT

FOR US, AS FOR MOST BUSINESSES, JUST OPENING IN THE morning is like being on land-mine patrol. Sooner or later, a mine will go off.

At our restaurants we serve hundreds of thousands of people a year. Realistically, we will upset a customer or two along the way. Even if we are 99.9 percent perfect, that means four or five times a day, we have a customer who is not entirely happy with us.

In my word-of-mouth-driven business, a mistake is devastating. Our average dinner check is $60 per person. If the average party is four people, then the average group is worth $240. If each of the four guests at the table tells ten people about a bad experience, and each of those ten people chooses not to go to Brennan's the next time they consider it, that single bad experience could cost us 40 tables worth $240 each—or $9,600. That doesn't account for potential repeat visits.

So yes, mistakes are a big deal. But worrying about the customer-service minefield can make your people nervous, uncomfortable and anxious and unable to do their best work.

Your team needs support systems and a methodical process to deal with the inevitable screwups. That kind of training serves as a powerful shield which not only protects your business but your employees. They can stop worrying constantly.

And it can be a relief for the owner, too.

PRIZE PATROL

"Gifts are like hooks."

— MARCUS VALERIUS MARTIALIS

One day as I sat licking my ego wounds after feeling a customer's wrath, it occurred to me that I was the only person who felt the pain of the complaint, and I had assigned myself, alone, the task of resolving the complaint and getting the customer back. I mean, I am the owner, and shouldn't the buck stop with me?

But I realized that employees should feel the pain along with management as well as become part of the solution. This led me to create one of the most important elements in our customer-satisfaction efforts.

Now, when we do screw up, we have a plan. We hold ourselves accountable, and we take extraordinary measures to make sure the customer knows how important he or she is to everyone at Brennan's of Houston. I call our plan an "overwhelming response," but my team has nicknamed it the Prize Patrol.

When we receive a complaint, first our managers review it. Then the offending party and every member of the service team is briefed. If the situation warrants, the Prize Patrol swings into action.

The Prize Patrol includes the executive or sous chef on duty the day of the offense, the manager who was on duty, and other members of the service team. The Prize Patrol — anywhere from three to ten people — drives to the home or office of the offended customer. They knock at the front door, their hats in their hands, their arms laden with flowers, a letter of apology, and boxes of our famous pralines.

Patrol members look the customer in the eye (just as they have been taught to do when a customer arrives at our restaurant), apologize sincerely for not creating a great customer memory. We ask the customer to give us another chance and present a gift certificate for a free dinner.

This method may sound extreme, but let me assure you, the customer gets the message that he or she is important. We have a 100 percent customer-return rate.

Do I have to hold a gun to the heads of the staff to make them do this? Not anymore. The staff doesn't look forward to going on Prize Patrol (who likes apologizing?), but they understand why we do it. Disappointing — or worse, losing — a customer devastates the staff as much as it does me. And keeping a customer under tough circumstances shows what an excellent organization we are. To my surprise, the Prize Patrol is one of our best pride-building techniques.

But don't just take my word for it.

ltress
erson,
r with
orders
t they
aiting
with-
led to
rote a
anage-
estau-
n cus-
offer
ses.

uston
nuch-
arket,
und it
tion of
e and
s his
ne re-
ng his
ng the
eir or-
didn't
as the
n. The
chef's
d have
them
ne only
asn't
onut-
hrimp,
opped
nger-
cream
ve, he
can be

Kitchen has been a favorite of hers for years.

Poor performance

Louis D. Lerner of Houston says he needed a special place to dine last week when his future in-laws were in town to celebrate the engagement of his daughter and their son. He selected the venerable **Brennan's**, 3300 Smith. But the party of 10 was shocked by inattentive, rude service. He had to ask for everything except the wine list, which was given to a guest rather than Lerner, the obvious host. None of the food arrived at the same time, and it seemed an eternity for everyone to be served. The caesar salad was bland, water-logged and not prepared tableside, as in the past. The soups were tasteless and barely warm. The beef had a line of gristle making it difficult to cut. T Flounder Veronique, a co r-less dish, was not worth its price. Brennan's signature dish of pecan-crusted, pan-seared fish was made with halibut, not the usual redfish or trout. The once-great performance of preparing bananas Foster was done by the water server, not the maitre d' or head captain, as in the past.

MEMORANDUM

Date: 08/21/2001

To: Whine and Dine

From: Louis D. Lerner

RE: Follow-up to Letter Run 8/10/01-"Poor Performance"

This is a follow-up letter to my previous complaints of Brennans Restaurant. I hope you share it with your readers, Brennans deserves it.

It was almost no sooner had your published letter of my complaints hit the morning coffee table, that I received a call from Matthew Henderson, of Brennans Restaurant. He wanted to go over my letter in detail, which we did for 30-45 minutes. He was very, very, apologetic, not only for the food and service short falls, but for, equally important, not making that evening memorable for us, for the right reasons. He couldn't have been more congenial. He said that while my letter got more than a little of their attention, he hoped it would serve as an opportunity for them to look closer at their operations and tweak them where needed.

I was assured that the experience we encountered was a blip on the radar screen that I should not, in fact, fear that Brennans had slipped to a common level of mediocrity. He wanted to put things right and quickly offered to comp the entire meal, which I assured him, was not my purpose in writing the original letter. He said that was the least he could do, but wanted to go a step further, with my permission. We arranged for him to come to my home the following day to personally deliver this "step further".

He arrived the next day with flowers in hand, two boxes of those famous Brennans pralines, and a gift certificate for our next meal at the restaurant. All of this was totally unbelievable; however, the thing that blew me away was that he had with him the entire wait staff on duty that night who were responsible for our table, including, our waiter, four assistant table servers, the manager in charge of the entire room that night, and lastly, to my amazement, two chefs from the kitchen! These chefs were not salad shredders either; one had 19 years' experience at Brennans alone. All were in attendance for the sole purpose of personally and individually, apologizing for our experience.

Now I must tell you that any business, **any business**, which goes to that extreme, must assuredly have the customer foremost in its approach to delivering the goods.

I must and will give Brennans a second chance to provide me with the memories missed on our last visit.

Louis D. Lerner

White Space Planning

"Time stays long enough for anyone who will use it."
— LEONARDO DA VINCI

MY LAST THOUGHT ON HUMAN NATURE IS ABOUT THE OWNER'S own human nature and how you manage yourself.

One day my calendar and my personal goals came up on the computer at the same time. Clicking back and forth, I noticed that almost none of my appointments had anything to do with getting me to where I had told myself I wanted to go. No wonder I was frustrated!

I could not cancel many of my appointments, deadlines or meetings because without them, the business might not go forward. Meetings with lawyers, accountants and other Indian chiefs are mandatory.

But there were a lot of meetings that weren't mandatory, and once I was honest with myself, I admitted they were there to fill up my day and make me feel as if I was making progress when all I was doing was creating activity.

The unnecessary meetings were devouring the time I should have been devoting to my personal goals and finding a better balance between work and family.

I realized then that my personal goals would have to be

accomplished in the "white space" on my calendar — that is, in that blank spaces between mandatory business appointments.

In large measure, I was solely to blame. My calendar looked the way it did because of the choices I had made. I filled my calendar because I was afraid of my own human nature; I was afraid I'd let procrastination creep in.

It was my choice to schedule the appointments; therefore, it was my choice to determine what I would do with the time in the white spaces. After a few minutes of reflection, I realized that if I kept my goals and my appointments together, I couldn't ignore my goals when I was filling in my daily schedule.

From that point forward, I became drawn to those white spaces. The opportunities between the necessary job appointments were time I could schedule to work on my goals. And if I could see progress, I would feel better about myself, as well as develop pride in knowing that I was doing my job.

In large measure, it was in the white spaces that I was able to write this book.

The white space became such a vital part of me that I shared it with my management team. Together we evolved the concept of "white space planning."

The obvious first barrier to adopting the process is the nagging self-question: How can I stay on track when I'm so busy and have so many interruptions and emergencies?

In many businesses, interruptions are a fact of life. (The restaurant business has been described as a series of interruptions.) But no matter their business, successful people must find a way to stay on course or get back on track when unscheduled interruptions take them off course.

At that moment of truth, you have to make a choice: Do I let life and my career just happen, or do I take control and decide where I am going?

There are many simple techniques to help you stay the course when you stumble, but they all boil down to doing the basics: Writing down your goals and scheduling your day according to your personal priorities.

In essence, you create a *daily game plan in accordance with your exciting goals* while everything you do remains focused on your customers. If you just walk in the door in the morning and start, it's almost impossible to make progress, no matter how much energy you put into it.

The best way to do this is to use the personal planning calendar that you carry with you and use daily. If you put your goals in the front or on the bookmark used to find the current date, you'll see them daily. Then if you take the time to input your busy times (important parties and other scheduled events like meetings or vacations) you'll automatically see the time you have left available to attack the goals that will keep you in your virtuous cycle.

It's just basic time management, but to be successful, you must commit to using this discipline, or time will get the best of you. It's the difference between leaving at the end of your day feeling as if you accomplished important things or feeling as if you spent the entire day putting out fires.

You'll be tired either way, but it's a great feeling when you see those goals accomplished. You'll feel good, and you'll keep it up. You can also schedule yourself back on track if you slip a bit. Time is your friend or your enemy. The choice is yours.

You Can Feel
It Working

"These are my principles, and if you don't like them... Well, I have others."
— GROUCHO MARX

IT IS SMALL MOMENTS AND QUIET VICTORIES RATHER THAN big brassy happenings that have made the journey worthwhile for me. I like seeing people grow as professional restaurateurs or rising from an entry-level position at minimum wage to a managerial position, then being able to buy a house. I like seeing the smiles of the cooking staff as I walk through the kitchen. You know when your system is working.

You know, too, when it's not. In spring, 2003, we had gotten cocky about ourselves and our ability to deliver the Simple Truth. We were put to the test on Easter, traditionally one of the busiest days of the year. We delivered a great meal with exceptional service that day, but inside, each of us felt that we had not given our all, or delivered our best.

On the Monday after Easter, I did not have to call a staff meeting or even go around and have a Simple Truth reminder meeting with my people. I could tell by their postures and the looks in their eyes that they knew what I knew: We had gotten by on our reputation and next time might not be so lucky.

Rather than beat ourselves, we picked ourselves up and recommitted ourselves to the Simple Truth. Our team went back to blocking and tackling. We couldn't wait till Mother's Day to prove we deserved our reputation and that we wanted to earn it every day.

That day, we served a staggering crowd, more than 1,200 people. The staff knew they had to deliver their best because every guest who walked through the door that day was there to create a special memory.

The day passed without a single negative comment from a customer! I enjoyed hearing our guests say how excellent their experiences had been. But even more, I enjoyed hearing my team tell me that we could have served hundreds more, and it would have not affected quality or the guest experience. By the end of the day, we were exhausted but victorious.

It is small moments like that when you know it's working. You won't find that feeling in surveys or studies, but you'll notice it in the smiles and voices of those who believed in you and bought into the journey.

I started on this journey out of frustration and desperation, knowing something had to give. When I began, I felt it was either going to be me or them, and that I was going to have to bring them around to see things my way. Funny thing is, I am the one who's been brought around the most.

And I am the one who has benefited the most. Well, me and about a million customers who have since left Brennan's of Houston with great memories!

Lagniappes

A Consultant Examines Brennan's Culture

BY LARRY TAYLOR

"Most of us never recognize an opportunity
until it goes to work in our competitor's business. "

— P.L. ANDARR

IN THE HORRIFIC COLLAPSES OF WORLDCOM, GLOBAL CROSSing, HealthSouth, Enron, Adelphia Cable and Tyco, many wonderful people lost their jobs and their pensions. (I live in Houston, and many of those folks are my friends.)

But these corporate implosions have been a boon for my consulting business. I used to run into unenlightened CEOs who said something like this: "Culture is that airy-fairy, touchy-feely, soft stuff that the HR director keeps bugging me about. My job is to build shareholder value and put bucks on the bottom line. I don't have time to mess with the culture."

I don't hear that line much anymore. The collapses of Enron, et al proved the bottom-line impact of corporate culture. Now, no board of directors or CEO can afford to ignore it.

I'm passionate about defining and building cultures. An organization's culture — its normative beliefs and behaviors — is the glue that holds the organization together under pressure.

It's the measuring stick by which all decisions are made. It is the moral and ethical compass that guides the organization's people. And it is a proven predictor of future performance.

Cultures built on greed, dishonesty, avarice and arrogance brought down Enron and the others. Those culture allegedly enabled — or even encouraged — their people to cook the books.

Academic studies show the flip side of the story. Positive corporate cultures yield higher profits. From 1979 to 1990, Harvard professors John Kotter and Jim Heskett studied 32 U.S. companies including General Motors, CitiCorp, General Electric and Hewlett-Packard to IBM, Sears, Xerox and Kodak.

In their book *Corporate Culture and Performance*, Kotter and Heskett reported that during that time period, the companies with constructive cultures far outperformed those with defensive cultures. The difference was dramatic:

	CONSTRUCTIVE	DEFENSIVE
REVENUE	682%	166%
STOCK PRICE	901%	74%
NET INCOME	756%	1%

The success of Commander's Palace in Las Vegas, combined with my observations of the day-to-day workings at Brennan's of Houston, provides strong anecdotal proof of Alex's Simple Truth philosophy. But I wanted to take the examination one step further. I wanted data to describe the difference in corporate culture that the Simple Truth can make.

For studying cultures, the best quantitative measurement tool I have found is the Organizational Culture Inventory®

(OCI), a survey developed by Human Synergistics International. Members of the organization respond to 120 statements about what is expected of the organization's members, that is, about the group's beliefs or behavioral norms. They're asked to what extent people in the organization are expected to do things such as "point out flaws," "be a 'nice guy,'" or "question decisions made by others." They answer on a scale of one to five.

Individual responses remain anonymous, but the organization's aggregate score is plotted on The Circumplex™ — basically, a circle divided, pie-like, into twelve slices. Each slice represents a cultural style. The styles are divided into three "factors:" Constructive, Passive/Defensive, and Aggressive/Defensive. Once plotted on the Circumplex, an organization's score can be compared to the normative responses of more than 700 organizations.

The Constructive styles (shown in blue) promote satisfaction behaviors and are generally the most conducive to an organization's success. The Circumplex has a bold ring indicating the 50th percentile. A simple way to read the circumplex is to remember that you want to see Constructive styles outside that bold ring, and to keep the Defensive styles inside it.

To test the Brennan's of Houston culture, I used the OCI in two ways. I asked one group of employees to respond to the 120 OCI statements from the perspective of the restaurant five years ago. A second group responded based on the culture today.

Here's the Circumplex showing what Brennan's of Houston was like five years ago:

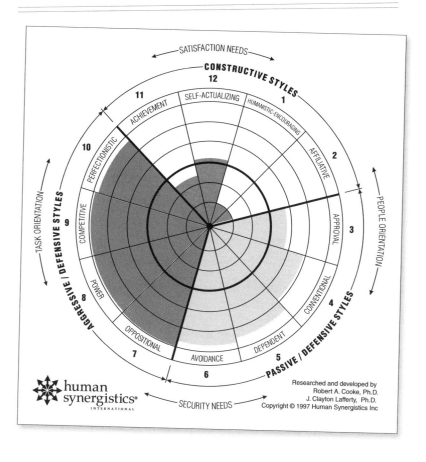

Researched and developed by
Robert A. Cooke, Ph.D.
J. Clayton Lafferty, Ph.D.
Copyright © 1997 Human Synergistics Inc

That culture was extremely Defensive. Almost no Constructive behaviors were rewarded or recognized.

Such a culture behaves like this:

☞ Being seen as large and in charge is more important that
being right or doing the right thing. Members believe they
will be rewarded for taking charge and controlling subordinates.

☞ The Perfectionist behaviors of setting unrealistic goals, pointing out flaws, avoiding mistakes and personally keeping track of everything results in an organization of demoralized people who are expected to work long hours to attain narrowly defined objectives.

☞ The Oppositional behaviors reinforce people who oppose the ideas of others and make safe decisions. Such behavior results in unnecessary conflict, poor group problem-solving and watered-down solutions to problems.

☞ The Avoidance and Dependence behaviors are usually subordinates' reaction to the strong power and control behaviors displayed by those in charge. Such organizations punish mistakes but fail to reward success and expect subordinates to clear all decisions with superiors.

This Circumplex makes it obvious that Brennan's of Houston was not a fun place to work. Due to quality food and a rigid delivery system that fortunately ran like a well-oiled machine, Alex managed surprising success. But the system could not tolerate variation or instantaneously respond to customer needs.

The second Circumplex represents today's Brennan's of Houston, whose culture is based on the Simple Truth. You can see a remarkable improvement over the old culture.

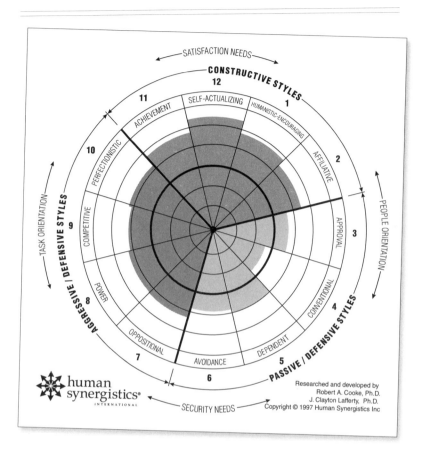

Researched and developed by
Robert A. Cooke, Ph.D.
J. Clayton Lafferty, Ph.D.
Copyright © 1997 Human Synergistics Inc

The Circumplex shows a little more Aggressive/Defensive styles than I'd like, but that style may be inherent to the restaurant business, which relies heavily on minimum-wage employees whose roles demand perfunctory adherence to a preparation and clean-up system. Taking that into account, Alex's culture is even stronger than this circumplex indicates.

And look how the Simple Truth has boosted Constructive styles!

The Self-Actualizing style forms the bedrock behaviors of a Simple Truth organization. Self-Actualizing organizations value creativity, quality over quantity, and both task accomplishment and individual growth. Members are encouraged to enjoy their work, develop themselves, and take on new and interesting activities. Self-Actualizing organizations tend to be innovative, offer high-quality products and services, and attract and develop outstanding employees.

The second most dominant Constructive style in Alex's organization is Humanistic-Encouraging. Such organizations are managed in a participative, person-centered way. Members are expected to be supportive, constructive and open in dealing with one another. This style provides for the growth and active involvement of members, who report high satisfaction with the organization, and deep commitment to it.

Based on strengths in Achievement and Affilitative, Alex's organization is also proficient at setting and achieving realistic goals, establishing plans to reach those goals, and pursuing them with enthusiasm. These styles promote open communication, good cooperation, and loyalty to work groups.

Based on my professional experience, I would state unequivocally that Alex's Simple Truth approach to building an organization works.

And in using the culture data to predict the future of the organization, I would say that Brennan's of Houston will be able to weather the ups and downs of the economy and the business cycle, and will continue to outperform the market — if Alex minds his P's and Q and doesn't forget the Simple Truth.

An Intimate Conversation with Alex and Ella

"Happiness is having a large, caring, close-knit family in another city"
— GEORGE BURNS

MY MOTHER, ELLA BRENNAN, IS A NEW ORLEANS LEGEND. SHE'S run Commander's Palace since the 1970's, and has been in the hospitality business since 1943, when my family owned the Old Absinthe House, and at the first Brennan's on Bourbon Street. She's known for her powerful charm, her mentoring, and for the legendary chefs she's given their start — among them, Paul Prudhomme, Emeril Lagasse and the late Jamie Shannon. I've learned a lot from her, but our styles are vastly different.

Recently we sat down to talk business.

ELLA: When I started I was a child, literally 17 years old, working for my older brother, who I thought walked on water. We each watched a door. He would bring the customers in the front, and I tried to keep all the profits from walking out the back. It really was that simple at the beginning.

As far as I was concerned, I was just as good as any man out there. But these people that came to work for us were mostly men, and they didn't understand that. I had no idea that would be a problem, and never acted like it was, and never let it be.

The restaurant business isn't easy. I fought people every day of my life in business. I wanted everyone to be their best, and I used to have to fight them to do it. I always felt, and still do today, that I or someone in the family had to be there. At first it was more about the back door because we had to babysit the business. I believed we had to be there to make the business as good as it could be because no one else was going to do it. It was sheer force of will back then.

I think that has changed over the past fifteen or twenty years, and it has really been in the last five or so that our team is just as committed as the family is to seeing that the business can be the absolute best in delivering what the customer wants. I guess that is what my son calls "great memories." I have always been blessed with good people, and one of the true joys in my life has been as a mentor. I have had some great pupils that have really gotten it and gone on to do their own thing.

ALEX: Mom, that's one of the real differences in what managing by the Simple Truth brings. In the past we felt we had to make all the important decisions. We eventually would run off those that really got what you were teaching because they wanted to do it for themselves, to be the ones making the calls. What really is happening now is by teaching and demanding that we stay aligned with our Simple Truth, everyone is able to make decisions and feel a significant part of the business. We're able to hold on to some of these folks longer as well as bring along some younger ones with more consistency.

ELLA: My smarter-than-his-mother son says, "We used to hire geniuses and fire idiots." And I supposed that it is true. That's why the really good ones stood out so much.

You really can't hire a good waiter. You have to hire a good person with a good personality and an attitude. If you can hire happy, anxious-to-make-you happy people instead of efficient robots, you're going to be better off in the restaurant business.

ALEX: I think many people leave Commander's feeling like they got more than they gave. That's why there's literally a club of ex-employees — "alumni" — around the country. They're proud that Commander's keeps pushing the bar higher.

ELLA: They come back from all over. It's one of the great rewards of my life.

ALEX: Dealing with employees now is different than when you started.

ELLA: For the better, I can tell you! There are fewer of those anxious-to-make-you-happy people, but we've learned to make them proud so they stay. We've tried to give them more a sense of professionalism.

ALEX: Right, but it's still tough to manage people even if they are more motivated and educated. People still behave in what they perceive as their own best interests, and you can't buck human nature. At best, you can only harness it.

ELLA: The opening in Las Vegas is what convinced me that this stuff could be taught. I was scared to death about hanging the name Commander's Palace in Las Vegas. What do those people know about Southern hospitality? That's my reputation they're dealing with. But they did it. Alex and Brad talking about the philosophy all the time sounded kind of silly at first, but it did work. I don't think there has been one review or article written that doesn't mention our people and the Southern hospitality atmosphere we have created.

ALEX: You were scared? I almost had a heart attack. The thought of the guests having more experience with Commander's than our average opening employee kept me awake many nights.

ELLA: The really exciting part has been to see how all these young people have embraced the Simple Truth. They really do use it all the time, and even the youngest seem to know this is what is expected.

You can have a restaurant that creates dining memories, and you don't have to be there all your waking hours. You can develop people who have the same felings and attitudes you do who can do that for you. You don't need to be there every waking hour.

ALEX: I think that is the beauty of the Simple Truth. In our New Orleans restaurants, we always had the B.O.D. — the Brennan On Duty. The B.O.D. way nearly killed me in Houston where there was just me. I had to find another way.

The clarity and simplicity of what the customer expects and our alignment and managing with the tide, not against it, is why the young people like it. I have had some say to me they did not know work could be like this, that they could enjoy it. They look at management and perceive nothing but people trying to control them and they balk at it. They get no sense of personal accomplishment out of work. When the Simple Truth is laid out for them and then you tell them to find their own way, they get that pride, probably something some of them have never had before. In fact, I define classic management as "the futile attempt to control that which is ultimately uncontrollable: human nature."

ELLA: You can tell my son is enthusiastic about this. And I didn't want him to go into the restaurant business. I wanted him to get a master's degree in something.

ALEX: Mom, you're the one that infected me. You taught my sister and me to read profit and loss statements when we were in junior high.

You are the best mentor I have ever seen. You were mentoring before it was cool!

ELLA: I had some wonderful people who looked out for me and taught me.

ALEX: Common sense and your voracious appetite for business books didn't hurt. My sister and I don't have to go out and search for the best business books. If it is any good, it will come to us dog-eared and underlined within a week of being published.

ELLA: I had my failures — [the Brennan's restaurants in] Atlanta and Dallas — and I learned a lot from them, too. Maybe I should have bought more books! But I think the real problem was that we just didn't have a family member to go there.

ALEX: I learned from that, too. The biggest lesson was that we must have key people who are committed as much as we are and will stay with us. Like you always said, "I don't want to pull anybody up the hill. I don't mind if they run along with me, or better yet ahead!

ELLA: You know, I think of family today as those that get it and are running with me or even ahead. That's more than just a last name, I'll tell you.

ALEX: Seriously, Las Vegas is where I started this whole thing of putting tradition down on paper and then determining what to evolve or change altogether from what we have always done. When I sat down to begin to write, I began with the concept that you have continually banged into my head, the concept of continual improvement, and why it is so important.

ELLA: As my old friend Helen Hayes said, "If you rest, you rust!" I've seen too many good restaurants and businesses ultimately fade and fail because they did not evolve. Evolve, I don't mean change. Change scares customers off. You can't do it fast. It almost needs to be imperceptible to them, as if it's always been this way, only better.

ALEX: That's called Restaurant Magic.

ELLA: I guess that's right. Like Aunt Adelaide used to say, "The restaurant business is like being on stage on Broadway, only we do matinees daily." Speaking of that, the curtain's going up, young man.

Plodding Is
Never Finished

WE WOULD LIKE TO HEAR FROM YOU, OUR CUSTOMER, WHETHER
our book met your needs. We would also like to hear from you if
you'd like to discuss how the Simple Truth and Plodding might
work in your business.

Please visit our web site, www.simpletruthbook.com.

Or you can write to us individually:

Alex Brennan-Martin, www.brennansofhouston.com

Larry Taylor, www.beanorange.com